Pink Flamingos and Wild Horses

Book Three of the Still Living His Dream Series

Still Blundering around in France

By Lisa Edgar-Powell

Chapter One

Casting off our Old Life

It seemed like we would never move our boat *Jantina*, on the day we were due to start our new adventure, *Matilda* our three-legged cat decided otherwise and disappeared for the morning. Yet again, were cruising to a deadline, the canal was due to close in two weeks for yearly maintenance and if we didn't get off it, we would be waiting a further month before we could go anywhere.

After searching the area and our friend Mick, joining in with his two dogs, which probably would have deterred her from returning, rather than encouraged as the two are killer dogs, in the nicest of ways, the dogs and our *Matilda*, only living nearby in perfect harmony with one or the other party locked away in the respective boats.

It was after lunch when we finally departed, *Matilda*, nonchantly strolling up to the boat and hoping on. We had decided to have some lunch and were enjoying the Midday, early Spring sun, warming our faces. When she arrived, we swiftly locked her inside and cast off the ropes.

This was our first experience or travelling with the cat aboard. We had started boating without any pets, by boat number 4, *Bilbo* our hairy black and white Welsh Fox Hound had become part of the crew, and now *Matilda*, our three-legged cat had joined us. This had never been part of the plan, and whilst mooring requirements had altered since *Bilbo* joined us, ultimately resulting in us swapping from our Dutch Cruiser to our live board Dutch Barge as *Bilbo* was too heavy to lift off the stern if we moored in port, *Matilda* was supposed to live with our daughter, until she decided to return to the Uk live.

Matilda brought a whole new set of constraints, with only three legs, she needed to be able to get off the boat safely, windows, doors and hatches needed to be closed, and so we would find out on the first day, extra time allowed to find her. She had been content living aboard until we moved, with a wood and a fabulous park to explore, she could roam freely. After an incident where she slid off the side of an abandoned plastic boat, dunking herself in the drink, she quickly learnt, not to hop from boat to boat. We soon found the pre-requisites of having our cat onboard took precedent over our requirements, it also meant I needed to get up earlier as inevitably she was not onboard when I returned from my dog walk, as Jeffrey, my darling husband, would open the door to start the morning moving checks and inevitably forget, I would return complaining *"I can't find Matilda"*, and I would crossly walk away with *Bilbo* muttering under my breath, "shut the ****** door ".

After all the fuss of the morning, we only travelled a short distance, managing one lock and mooring, but I suppose at least we made a start. It would be one of many times, our plans were scuppered, because of our sweet *Matilda*.

I wondered whether *Matilda's* reluctance to leave was an echo of our feelings. The last couple of weeks had been manic. When we returned from our second visit to Spain for the winter, we set about getting the boat ready to leave but I had heaps of paperwork that had arrived regarding the closure of our French business. Our home had been sold the previous October, but we still seemed to have bills arriving in our name, it was not a new start, with French Bureaucracy chasing our tails. Our daughter had dropped the bombshell on our return that she was quitting French University at the end of the course year and returning to England, which threw us in a quandary. Firstly, the idea had been we were cruising in the country she lived in and would catch up with her during all the holidays, secondly, if she left France, we would not have an address, as the apartment we were renting for her was currently our French address.

We had emotional and practical issues to tackle. We had a car and a caravan we had just bought, registered at the apartment, we had until the end of May to get a new French address. When we sold our home, we had not foreseen any problems as we had signed a three-year lease for the apartment and who knew where we would be in three years, I certainly didn't.

Unsure of our future, while The Daughter was applying to Universities in England, I was making full use of the healthcare system that we had contributed to for the last ten years. Having cancelled our health insurance (you need to pay a top up in France, for the excellent service that everyone hears about), I had cancelled ours in December when we closed the company down but was delighted to find that there was a period we were still covered for. Consequently, I had booked in all my yearly appointments to take place before we left, as we were still only a 40 minute away from the old town that we had lived in for ten years.

I was sad to say farewell to my doctor, over the years I had tried to teach him some basic words of English to use when stray boaters wandered into his office and as our daughter had been friends with his, it was the small-town community feel that many of us yearn for. Unlike the computerised systems of the Uk, where you type your date of birth into a computer and then when your appointment flashes up, appointments made online, with our busy town surgery, I would telephone to make an appointment, the receptionist (there were two) would greet me a Bonjour Madame Powell, for you or Emily?

It is strange to think that the things I scoffed at when we first moved to France as old fashioned and provincial, I would now have appreciated and would miss. Although, I never felt part of the community, somehow, we had become absorbed into it, without realising. It is only now, when I am spending hours online and on hold to a well-known insurance company that I crave for the simplicity of telephoning my local AxA agent, Cyrille, and the girls in the office (whose names I knew and whom I bought chocolates for at Christmas) responding with a) Bonjour Lisa, and B) A response to the problem. Perhaps living in 70's France, isn't so bad after all.

The last week before we left, our daughter came to spend her birthday, little did I know, it would be the last one we spent with her for years. The next time we would see her it would be the Easter holidays, and hopefully we would be in St Jean de Losne, a town that she had spent many hours in, in various boats. For her, it was also a farewell to *Matilda*, as the decision to move to the Uk meant that she could no longer keep her in the apartment, I am not sure who she was sadder to be parted from. With her returned to her home in Nancy, we set about stocking up the boat and I had the fun of buying a rod licence for my husband. You may ask why he didn't get his own license, there are two responses to that. Firstly, my French is far superior to his, which doesn't say a lot, unless you are talking, fishing, boating or DIY, his language repertoire. Secondly, from very early on, I have always been the organised one. Having quit my job in London temporarily as Manager of a renowned fashion chain, to set up an office for his fledgling company, 13 years later, I was still there. Although, the role had changed over the years as the company grew, my necessity to organised him, never ceased. Some 25 years later, and another business down the line, while he makes sure the boat has fuel, I make sure the boat has insurance and a yearly licence! Which is why, I took the test for the VHF licence that we needed for the boat, which has proved very useful, when spending hours on the phone to customer services, using my phonetic alphabet, after taking years to learn how to pronounce the vowels in our name in French.

Departing Froncles, was our final goodbye to our old life, the last piece of familiarity, the white whiskered old chap with the flat cap, who stopped to pet *Bilbo*, every morning, when we crossed the bridge, joking that if I wasn't going to use him as a hunting dog, he would happily have him. The French couple in the motorhome, with their two little dogs, that arrive the second week of March every year, setting up until October, their friends joining them for petanque most afternoons and a barbeque at weekends. The guys that worked at the local VNF offices, where *Bilbo* would stop every morning for a stroke before we carried on with our walk, and Valerie, our lovely Capitain, who was never without a smile, and nothing was too much trouble. Like living in our village, these people had become our everyday, as had we, the funny English people, with the scruffy black and white dog, on the big boat. We waved farewell to the soft green hills and the clean damp air as we had done many times before, but this time, we weren't coming back.

When we stopped on our first short day, I was filled with sadness, we had left behind Mick and his two dogs, and our friends in port due to arrive, Richard with his beautiful and dog *Amber*, and Deidre and Michael, the co-owners of *Beau*, or old boat and we were travelling alone, our last roots in France gone.

The following morning, the sun shone through the early morning mist, causing little particles of water to sparkle like glitter. we set off to Chaumont, and I felt much more cheerful, filled with anticipation for the journey ahead. I would like to say that the day went swimmingly, but at the first lock, I put three ropes on as the water gushing in seemed a bit fierce, and all three snapped. It appeared that the harsh winter temperatures that they had been exposed to had caused them to deteriorate, that and perhaps I had put them on too tightly. It had been eighteen months since we had done any locks and it always takes a few days to get into the swing of things, after buying *Jantina* and bringing her from Holland, we had just got to grips with her when we moored up and got on with the rest of life, selling our home and business so we could start on the big adventure, the top of French boating bucket lists The Rhone and The Canal du Midi.

We hadn't even managed a full days cruising and we had already broken three ropes, good start. As the day wore on, the temperatures lowered, and the wind increased, and we remembered what the weather was supposed to be like in March, scuddy clouds and a darkening sky. We moored up in Chaumont, the first time we had ever got a mooring spot there, I took *Bilbo* off for a walk and we settled inside with the heating on, our time for leaving in the morning booked with the lock keeper as he needed to open the lock for us.

Sometime later, we heard an engine and Jeff hopped off to help the owners moor up. They were travelling in a sail boat, so a little wind wouldn't have phased them but when it's cold, it's always nice to have some help so you can get inside quickly. I stayed indoors and when my frozen husband returned, he informed me that the couple were American, and coming for drinks later that evening to discuss a strategy. They were booked in at a different time to us, but we felt that the lock keeper would want us to go in together to save water, we were a little concerned as to our proficiency, as we had not, yet, shared a lock with another boat, since the massive locks in Holland, two seasons earlier. We felt it was not the time to start, with a beautiful sailboat in front of us.

I attempted a quick tidy up, took *Bilbo* for a second walk to tire him out, as he tends to get overexcited with visitors, and then there was a tap at the door. Bill and Karen, the Americans, entered, carrying huge containers with straws. We evidently didn't need to provide any drinks and I was intrigued as to the contents of their supersize cups. Perhaps they were tee total? The last time we had dinner with some Americans they had admonished us for ordering a drink for our teenage daughter, we knew she wouldn't drink it, but it is normal practice in France.

The puzzle was rapidly solved, the voluminous cups contained vodka and slimline tonic, hence the reason they had brought their own. Phew! I later discovered this was a popular low-calorie tipple, and started to keep some tins of slimline tonic aboard, I was still intrigued to know, quite how much those cups held, and amused that there was a moment to pop back for a top up, to replenish the ice, something I definitely didn't have in March but something that Brits working in the service industries would always associate with Americans, the desire for ice in drinks.!

Generalisations over, we set about discussing and route and made plans for the rest of the week as we were all travelling to the same destination. After several hours, the conversation moved onto more general terms when suddenly a remark made by Bill brought the realisation that we had met before. Some years previously, our old boat *Maranatha,* had been moored in our home town of Vitry le Francois and we took to stopping off on our way home from visiting our clients at our fishing lake, to check the security of the boat. It was on one such occasion, that a sail boat was moored at the end of the port. The port was closed for winter without any amenities available and Jeff had walked over to the boat to offer assistance. The two men had a chat and whilst Jeff checked over our boat, Bill, a keen advocate for the I Phone, shown me some usual tricks, it was this particular moment that I had remembered, and he said, yes, that's my way of breaking the ice with people!

How strange that, all that time later, we would meet again. An enjoyable evening was had, and they departed before us the next morning, keeping in touch along the route, advising us of where there was space to moor etc and any problems along the way. We would catch up when we arrived.

We left after them and had a relatively uneventful journey, but as the locks were assisted, it was necessary to book every morning when you were leaving, and where you were stopping. As we don't possess a crystal ball, that wasn't the easiest thing, even with Karen and Bill's info. On one of the days, we told the lock keeper we would stop at a mooring we had used many times before, Foulain, and when we arrived the mooring was full, but the lock keeper had departed. We were left with no alternative but to continue to the next lock and telephone the lock keeper, who was more that slightly annoyed that we had had to call him out. As the week progressed the temperatures seemed to get colder. I felt like I was going skiing, I had so many layers on. By the weekend we decided to stop Saturday and Sunday as the locks were still assisted and there was a Formula One Grand Prix on that we wanted to watch on TV, which we would miss if we carried on as we would have been in the middle of a tunnel when it was due to be broadcast. What we were not party to, was the information that a fishing match was due to take place that weekend, at the very spot we had chosen to moor.

As I opened the door that morning, in search of the nearest boulangerie, I was greeted by rows of anglers with their fishing tackle set up along the banks next to us and opposite. It took a long time to get to the boulangerie, a chorus of *Bonjours* as I passed each way and *Bilbo* poking his nose into the buckets of bait laying beside them. I don't know if they caught any fish, as it was far too cold to watch them, but they left lots of rubbish all over the bank, which I ended up collecting, before it blew into the canal and suffocated a duck, or got stuck in a boats propeller.

One of the advantages of travelling the same canal many times, is that you have favourites places to moor, but out of season, less boats are moving, and more spaces taken up with boats, wrapped up under tarpaulins for the winter. Although it is frustrating to plan to stop somewhere and not be able to, it also allows discovery of new places. One such stop, which was new to us, a tiny village off the canal filled me with delight, so we didn't have a boulangerie, but we did find a magnificent bathing area constructed in a small building lay a shallow pool and outside a running well. A hidden treasure.

We were keen to get to the end of the canal, memories of not having any phone signal from previous trips and no facilities open in March were an enticement to move as quickly as possible. We had almost reached the end when we arrived at Maxilly sur Saone, the first time we ever moored in the dark, not much fun, but a series of delays brought us to our last point at 7.30 in the evening. We had made it to the last stretch, despite the lock keepers constant reminders that the canal was due to close. We were a little concerned as we had met a couple, years earlier, who had been on a canal due to close, when they got to two days before the end and were told they had to turn around and go back and come off a different canal as their chosen route had closed earlier.

The next problem we may encounter was the river Saone, known to flood at both ends of the year. We had experience ourselves of arriving in St Jean de Losne to take our old boat *Beau* onto the river but having to leave it in the harbour for another month as the river was flooded.

We left the safety of the canal on a Saturday morning and moored up in a familiar town, Pontailler sur Saone., I love the Hotel de Ville that overlooks it and the 19th Century washhouses tucked away, and I had been looking forward to getting to Pontailler as the walks along the river are divine, as are the cakes in the boulangerie. Having spent my late teenage years in Stratford upon Avon, and my first job placement sending me to Chester, I spent many hours reflecting by the river, before a dog to keep me company, I would settle down under a tree and pull out my book and expel my teenage angst writing poetry. I love canals, but the open expanse of rivers hold freedom to me.

Although Pontailler is a small town, they all having something to offer, if only I was brave enough to go and explore. Pontailler has an 18th Century Church, St Maurice, conveniently situated near to the boulangerie, perhaps I will make the effort. We tied up, but the winds were already strong, and I struggled to walk *Bilbo* around the park him getting over excited, in what I call "Yampy dog mode" something that occurs when it is windy, and he runs about erratically, dragging me with him. Returning to the boat I noticed that the wind had blown our automatic satellite dish over. Jeff, then climbed onto the roof of the boat, holding precariously onto a flimsy bar with the radio antenna on, whilst I pressed a button to make it rotate, we finally managed to get the dish to go flat, the safest option, for both, we were moored on a fast-flowing river, a man climbing about who can't swim, in high winds.

Later that day, the heating seemed to stop working. I was seriously considering how wise our decision to move onto the barge had been. Other people thought we were nuts, perhaps we were!

The winds were too high to travel, so we remained for the weekend, rain lashing down. The mooring is on concrete steps on the river was lapping over the top, threatening to flood. In the meanwhile, Jeff, spent hours online looking at information on the heating system. When we had purchased the boat, the previous owner had kindly provided spreadsheets on every tin of paint, lightbulb and filter required and labelled them accordingly. All manuals were filed in folders, household and otherwise. By the end of the weekend, I had remembered that there were also copies of downloaded manuals on a laptop that he had supplied. I had put it in a cupboard as it had a GPS system on it with Maps for Holland and Belgium but as there weren't any for France, it was obsolete, or so I thought.

After waiting an age for it to boot up, I scrolled through the files, and found a copy of the heating manual, printed it off, and gave it to The Husband to peruse. Within five minutes, he had the heating working again. The reason that it had stopped working, was not a hugely technical one, he had accidentally closed the fuel pipe to the heating when transferring fuel from one tank to the other. Relived that the heating was working again, I thought it best not to discuss the events, as he was feeling rather foolish, should the heating ever not work now, the first thing I ask him, is if he has been filling up the tank, but I don't think either of us will forget that again!

Waving goodbye to Pontailler, we didn't have any brocante to report, funfairs, wedding parties, or frog's legs for dinner that we had experienced on previous visits, we surmised that we really must cruise in the summer. Our next stop, also on the river Saone, was at Lamarche sur Saone. In our years of boating, we hadn't ever managed to get a space to moor there, even with our first ten metre boat. The reason that we wanted to stay was that the area was known as particularly good spot for fishing, the motive for buying our very first boat, and obviously our two last businesses. On one trip returning from the South by car, we had decided to book into a Chambre d Hote in the area as a stop over as we still had three hours before we got home. The Chambre d' hote was in a fantastic location, with its conservatory overlooking the Saone, we had enjoyed an A' l carte dinner but found ourselves heading up to bed at nine in the evening as the restaurant closed and we couldn't go outside! Not one of our better decisions. On another occasion, we had passed the village and noticed a sign with *A Vendre,* For Sale. The house was in a great position, with its garden backing onto the river with a small boat tied up. Our business minds where whirling away, and we wondered if perhaps we could buy it and run holiday lets for anglers, as we already had a holiday business in France. We drove around the village looking for the house and came upon the street that we thought it must be in and sat in the car spying from safety. A lady then came out of the house, saw us looking at it and tapped on the car door and asked us if we wanted to look inside. Sheepishly, we thanked her and followed her In, well it would have been rude not to.

The house was ghastly inside, had we never been inside a French house, we probably would have balked at it, but we had experienced some rather outlandish properties over the years, in various state of repair, this one seemed reasonably intact, but the interior so dark and poky that demolition seemed the only option. The outside, however was idyllic, could this be a possibility? We thanked her for her time and drove away. Several kilometres along the road we agreed, no, we would never persuade anyone to come to this godforsaken village in the middle of nowhere and put it to the back of our minds.

We had stopped for lunch at the mooring in Lamarche once, I had taken *Bilbo* for a quick wee and a man had shouted at me. I don't deal with confrontation very easily and had urged Jeff to depart rapidly. Perhaps it had been a private mooring, but there wasn't a sign, there were bollards, but these things get lost in translation, especially when a man with a shotgun, and a big dog are not happy.

We approached, what we hoped was the actual mooring, at speed. The wind was blowing us across the river and the rain was coming down in sheets. As the boat came alongside, I jumped off to secure the lines and got soaked through. A couple in a motorhome were parked in front of the mooring and watched with smug amusement as I struggled, being blown sideways whilst trying to pull the lines through. Previously I would have gone inside after getting drenched but now we had a hairy companion it was necessary to drag him out, so he too could get saturated and drip water all over the floor on his return. At least *Matilda* had enough sense to not want to go out!

In between bursts of rain, *Bilbo* and I managed to locate the local shop and take a walk around the village, some five years since our house hunting expedition, nothing had changed, I think that something had closed down, but other than that it was exactly the same. The boulangerie was closed for a month, for no apparent reason, the only business that seemed to be open normal hours was a florist specialising in funeral arrangements, something that I think I would have been looking for, had we opted to buy a property here.

It did appear that there was a lot of angling activity as we were woken at six the following morning by two old men, setting up their fishing tackle either side of our boat but the weather conditions did nothing to entice The Husband, to get his tackle out, or me.

After a brisk walk, around a public fishing lake, more our type of fishing, we returned to the boat to carry on our way, with a place mentally marked to return to at a later date, perhaps by car.

We arrived at Auxonne, with only the satellite dish not working, but with greater problems to worry about. The river was flowing rather fast and the wind was not letting up.

Auxonne has a fabulous port, but it also has some pontoons which were, as it was out of season, was vacant and empty. As *Matilda*, the cat, had not been able to go out for a few days, due to being moored on a quay directly onto the river, we were keen to moor somewhere safe for her. The pontoons in Auxonne were not ideal, but she seemed satisfied with sitting outside the boat, watching the ducks, the unpleasant weather, not encouraging her to explore further. She had not taken to cruising, as soon as the engine started, she would run into the bedroom and hide under the bed, venturing out after a couple of hours and settling on a chair, until we started to moor, as the low revs of the engine, and our bow thruster, which rotates and allows the bow to swing in, is reasonable noisy. She had taken to creeping out and trying to launch herself off, whilst we were trying to pull the boat in tightly. We quickly learnt to close the door properly behind us during this procedure, as the half door, which we thought would keep her in, she sussed out how to open. Cats are not stupid animals, it is their owners that are the problem.

We intended on staying in Auxonne for a few days, Auxonne is a great town, has some fabulous buildings and a bronze statue of Napoleon in its square. I am not convinced as to why statues of Napoleon are proudly shown in France, to me it is the equivalent of having a statue of Hitler in pride of place, but I am not French, and Jeff tried to extract from a French acquaintance of ours at a party years previously, why the French are proud of Napoleon when he wreaked so much havoc but couldn't get a sensible response, I am unsure as to whether it was the amount of alcohol consumed or the subject topic that rendered this normally eloquent man, speechless or the genuine instilled belief that he was a good man for France, but should you wish to see a statue of Napoleon, Auxonne has a very good one.

For me there were livelier French men that I was happy to observe. The Territorial Army have their barracks in Auxonne, and my morning dog walk, took me invariably passed a group of fit young men doing their training. The same barracks, of medieval pink Moissey stone were once the barracks of said young Napoleon, who was attending the local Artillery School, which can be found on the Northern side of Auxonne. His period there, he occupied two rooms successively and are now the 511th Logistic Regiment. As the Charlie Hebdo attack had only been the previous winter, it made me feel a bit safer staying somewhere with such a strong military presence. In fact, the only plus side of our daughter moving back to the Uk was she would no longer be living in the centre of a city in France. Going to university on high security alert was not something I would cherish and perhaps this had been part of her decision to move back after ten years of school in France.

Auxonne had enough to keep any keen tourists occupied, The Church of Notre Dame, a Civil and Military Hospital ,1862 Ramparts on the South Side of the town, and yes, more Napoleon memorabilia, in the Bonaparte District with the tower of Auxonne housing, a hat, set square and fencing foil that had belonged to him. Not something I would rush to see, but you can't complain of a lack of historical and architectural delights.

We had stayed in Auxonne on more than one instance, and seen the sights in warmer and more inviting temperatures but my morning walks allowed me to refamiliarize myself and discover new nooks and crannies. I really don't like being in marinas as I feel hemmed in, as all you can see is other boats, our mooring was on the river, opposite the rowing club, the young locals practising their skills, an occasional oar banging the side of the boat as they lost their bearings, and grabbed onto us, or pushed themselves off.

After a consultation with the Captain of the port, we established that there wasn't anyone who specifically fixed/installed satellite dishes and he suggested I approach a company in town who did home installations. Thinking that this was unlikely to work, I trotted off into town and made an appointment for a few days' time, our daughter was due to arrive the following week and I was keen to get it repaired before then.

The day the man arrived, it was extremely windy, and I was more than slightly concerned as to his safety. He climbed up onto the roof and held on for dear life. After replacing the LNB to no affect, he decided to come inside the boat and look at the equipment. After some fiddling about, he ascertained the problem, a fuse had blown. As the system had tried to realign itself in strong winds the dish had turned around and around and obviously overheated. It was the second time in two days we had felt a little foolish. A new fuse, and we had TV again and most importantly, the news, there was a general election the following month and we had been following events closely. There was also another Grand Prix the following weekend, the beginning of the season always exciting.

With the satellite firmly down, as the winds had not desisted, we holed up inside and later that afternoon, we were joined on the pontoon by an English couple in a Broads Cruiser, which is not a heavy boat. We moved up, as we had positioned ourselves in the centre of the pontoon to balance the weight evenly as our barge weighs 50 tonnes. Satisfied that we were reasonably moored we went inside for dinner, but as the evening drew on my husband decided to go outside and re do all the ropes, at the same time the other couple were outside doing the same thing. It seemed that every two hours we were back outside. They departed the following morning, to go to St Jean and we moved our boat back into the middle of the pontoon again, the wind had been scissoring behind our boat all night and I hadn't slept a wink, terrified that we, and perhaps the whole pontoon would come adrift in the river. Jeff then caught the train to Froncles, to collect our car, and I had an afternoon to myself, albeit not peaceful, as I kept running outside to check the ropes!

Our daughter arrived on the train the following evening and we were able to cast off and head for St Jean with her driving the car, on look out for a mooring, the first part of our journey over and the last part of our journey that was familiar to us.

March Cruising

Chapter Two

Familiar Territory

After what seemed like an interminable amount of bad weather, I had begun to wonder what possessed us to set off in March. We had travelled the same route, several times at the same time of the year, in boats not as adequate, yet this journey I had suffered with the weather, feeling cold and out of sorts throughout the journey, perhaps the realisation that this was the life we had chosen made it seem less of a holiday, more of a trial, but enjoy it, I did not. It was a relief to arrive in the small town of St Jean de Losne, a place we had spent many summers and stop for a while.

St Jean de Losne, sits on thirty-six acres of land and has twenty acres of water, with two marinas and one of the biggest hire boat bases in France, hotel barges, trip boats and a boating school, it is the mecca of the French waterways. As it is possible to join canals and rivers taking journeys all over France. It also has facilities to lift boats in and out of the water and workshops, so people can easily spend a whole summer there working on their boat and not go anywhere, but for us, it was our summer stop off. We had first visited in our first boat, where friends set up camp next to us, returned with a boat full of French teenager girls, not to be repeated, and friends with their children, and it was where we said goodbye to two of our boats through the brokerage, and over the years, many new friends. Although a small town, the restaurants and cafes overlooking the river and the Musee de la Battelleire and the St Jean Baptiste Church with its brightly coloured tiled roof, common in this region are part of the draw, sit in a bar long enough and you will hear a voice, not in French, ordering a café or a beer. I have not found anywhere like it in France, where the town is overtaken for six months of the year, yet retains its charm and originality.

Having moored up on the river frontage steps, surely the best position, in the town, we settled in for a few days. After another night on the sofa bed in the wheel house by The Daughter, and a morning spent moaning at her to move as we needed to access the storage areas below we decided to drive to Dijon, twenty-five kilometres from St Jean and purchase a fold up fishing bed, similar to the ones we had manufactured, so that the furniture could remain in place throughout her visits. As the weather had improved considerably, it doubled as a sunlounger during the day, but the temperatures had soared and none of us could stand to lie in the sun for more than half an hour.

Notice had been given on The Daughters apartment, and she had set about the task of clearing it out whilst studying so a few days lounging around was just what she needed. After the Easter break, we were to drive her back and transport and remove some of her belongings she no longer required to the *dechetterie*, the French municipal tip and the clothing recycling bins, as she didn't have use of a car.

On our first evening mooring, The Daughter, called me to tell me there was a lady talking excitedly outside the boat, wearing a bicycle helmet. I realised it was our American friend Karen, who cycled everywhere and unlike the less than safety conscious French, always wore a helmet. She invited us round to their boat for a drink that evening, and checking with The Daughter that she didn't mind being left on her second night, arranged to pop round early evening, gate code to the marina, in hand.

Having spent the last month in thermals, then gone straight into shorts and t-shirts mode, I was delighted to have an opportunity to try and pop on a dress, a trade mark scarf and suede boots and I walked with a swing in my step. Had there been music playing it would have been West Side Story's "I Feel Pretty ".

As we approached the marina, we looked for the correct numbered pontoon, I tapped in the code, and as we passed the first boat, saw the couple that had left us a few days earlier in Auxonne. After a quick chat, we explained where we were moored and arranged for them to pop over the following evening for a drink and then excused ourselves, lest we be late for our hosts. After an hour or so baking in the sun, we had discussed our varying experiences of the trip, since we had parted and our plans for the near future.

Suddenly, a head popped over and we were greeted with a

"Hello, I thought I recognised that voice"

The boat moored next to our friends, belonged to a couple we had met on the last good day of the previous season, when we were moored in Froncles. They were passing through and we had been sitting on the deck, enjoying the last hours of sunshine when they arrived. My Mother and step father had visited that day, after spending the weekend in Nancy, where our daughter lived, then bringing her for a visit before they departed back to the Uk. We had started drinking champagne at 11 am, far too early for us, as they wanted to have lunch and leave, and we were feeling rather exhausted, as I had been up making the boat ship shape before their arrival. The Daughter was inside, recovering after a Freshers week event and didn't actually meet them but the next morning, they had left quite late as we were all chatting on the quay. What a strange coincidence, there are hundreds of boats, in two marinas, and on one pontoon, we had already met three of their owners!

We departed after a pleasant evening, another social event planned. The following morning, an English barge arrived, and The Husband went out to help moor. St Jean de Losne is not an easy place to moor as it has large metal rings that you need to get the ropes through and they are set quite far back so assistance is always well received, usually as you may have a hire boat or a speed boat, bashing past you, knocking you a kilter whilst you are trying to do it.

A couple of hours later, there was a knock tap on the door and the owner asked if anyone spoke English, there was problem with the satellite system, a part had been ordered, and he was trying to track it down. *Lisa the Linguist* was surplus to requirements as we had onboard someone that could actually speak French as opposed me babbling along. The Daughter soon established the whereabouts of the parcel and we had a nose round the boat, as it was a much sought-after brand, the couple being the parents of the owner, who manufactured the boats. They had brought it to St Jean to participate in an exhibition in a couple of weeks. After much chatting, we invite them onboard later that evening, the other couple were coming, but it is quite a normal thing to do in boating circles, that's how you get to know everyone.

The evening was quite amusing, the first couple arrived, our daughter joining them, as unlike English teenagers, she had been brought up in France, where it is normal to mix with adults. After an hour or so, they departed, for dinner and within five minutes the other coupled joined us. I could see we would never leave St Jean, with such entertainment, in towards the end of the evening, my mobile rang, it was our friends from New Zealand, Bruce and Karen, calling for a chat. We had met them two years previously in St Jean de Losne and they had travelled with us on our maiden voyage with *Jantina*, having lots of fun along the way. They were now back home, planning a wedding for their son, with a new boat, but missing their boating in France.

The following morning, I was across the way from the laundrette. Although I have my own washing machine and dryer, I quite liked using the laundrette, as you ended up having a chat with other boaters, and it got me away from the boat for half an hour. I had only been there for about five minutes, when The Husband arrived and urged me to return. The gendarmes were on our boat, doing an inspection, I need to show them our papers!

Although this was our fifth boat, it was the first that we ever had inspected. One of our old boats, had an inspection when the new owners took it for a day trip along the canal, complete with underwater divers, and the owners had been featured in the local paper. I think it was a training exercise, but rather scary when you don't know what they want, I am sure.

I hurried back, aware that our fire extinguishers were out of date, as were our life jacket cartridges, we had intended on getting them all "done "before we set off on our big journey at the local chandlery as that was the first stop along the route. I panicked, the result of watching too many war films, where you are required to show your papers, but fortunately, we had our secret weapon on board, still in her pyjama shorts. Our voluptuous daughter immerged from the galley and offered to translate. They told her what we needed to replace and assured them that we would order new ones that day. When she had finished, the Gendarmes moved onto the English boat, and she hopped onboard and helped them. Had she not been there, I think we would have all been in a pickle as I am not a busty twenty-year-old, sadly.

With everything in order, it was apparent we were going nowhere fast as the new fire extinguishers were at least a week's delivery but with our receipt to show the gendarmes we had ordered everything, technically, we could not move the boat, which has convenient as the mooring is for three days only, and it was our second day when they visited us. By the weekend, as the weather had picked up, the town was busy. The restaurants were bustling, and The Daughter and I were catching up on some reading in the sun. It would have been the perfect weekend, had it not been for a little problem.

That morning, our daughter had dropped a tampon into the toilet, and flushed it away, or so she thought. Having been half asleep, despite spending years on boats and lakes with septic tanks, she had forgotten. It was not a simple task, our last boat had two toilets, so if one stopped working there was a spare, although in three years, we didn't have any problems, except when we closed a pipe in the winter, and forgot to open it the following Spring! With one toilet, not being moored in a marina with facilities, it was necessary to deal with it immediately. Our toilet was a particular type called a Macerator, which effectively, chops stuff up. Said tampon was stuck in the blades and had of course expanded. After denying that she had done it several times, she eventually owned up, so there was nothing for it, the toilet had to come out completely and be taken apart.

A very disgruntled husband set about disassembling it whilst I cleared the deck. It took four hours, the manual was in Italian, and it was in short, disgusting. While it was out on deck, tools thrown around, various friends popped over to say hello, and then left rapidly. Luckily, we were moored far enough away from the restaurants to not be in view, not what you want to see over Sunday Lunch!

When the job was done, The Husband reassembled it and put it back, then I suggested The Daughter and I left him alone. The Grand prix was about to start so we took *Bilbo* for a walk. In St Jean is a small housing estate, which we would walk passed to get to the port on the other side of the town.

As we approached the beginning of it, a small dog, similar to a Yorkshire Terrier appeared from nowhere. We thought it was quite cute and wondered where it had come from, it seemed to be following us and when we couldn't shake it off we turned around and walked back the way we came so that we didn't lead it away from it home to get lost. Instead it followed us all the way back to our boat! There are several old ladies that sit on the benches situated along the river every day, with their dogs that live locally, and I asked them if they knew who the dog belonged to but they didn't, and offered no assistance. I wanted to bring the dog on the boat until we contacted someone as cars drive along the river frontage, and I was concerned that it would get run over, but The Husband wasn't keen, so we took *Bilbo* back out and tried to lose it in front of the playing fields by the flats. Eventually, it trotted off and we left swiftly.

After lunch, we resumed our position on the deck and watched the comings and goings on the river. In front of us, a hire boat approached, and several people jumped off the boat to tie up. A man fell off and hit his head on the concrete steps. As they were positioned in front of one of the restaurants, whose veranda overlooked the steps. Someone called the pompiers, and soon the street was blocked off with ambulances and pompiers (fire men), they obviously didn't have a lot of emergencies as it seemed that they had all come out for one man, as he was stretchered off, I noticed the little dog had returned and was begging under the tables for scraps. People were shooing it away, and it was running from table to table. I took it upon myself to approach one of the pompiers and asked if it was possible they could take the dog away to safety, before it was run over in the chaos, but they were not interested. Despondent I returned to the boat, I had done all I could. Ironically, two years we returned to St Jean, and whilst out walking *Bilbo* and I saw the dog, in the same place, it was obviously very resilient I had been worried for nothing.

Later in the week, after depositing The Daughter back to her apartment for her to start selling the furniture from her apartment on Le Bon Coin, the equivalent of Gum Tree, we moved onto the canal to free up the mooring for others, but not before joining our neighbours for a drink in the local bar, before their boat went into port to be made spick and span for the exhibition.

Before we left, with our daughter's departure, we had invited some friends for dinner. As perchance, all the boats moored along the quay were English, with the exception of one Australian boat. People were starting to come out of the harbours and spending a few days on the river before they headed off for the season. Our friends arrived early and were talking to a couple on one of the other boats and I was talking to someone in front of her boat. To the side of us a French man was fishing, his rods set up behind our boat. Suddenly, we heard an engine noise and a hotel barge came careering towards us, everyone on the quay then sprang into action. The boat was out of control, the French man, shouting that if they hit his rods he would want compensating, and us shouting to slow down. They were going far too fast and trying to get into a space that wasn't big enough and heading straight for our bow. Hotel barges usually moored on the other side but there wasn't any space and boats that big are not allowed to moor at this specific mooring. Eventually, the man with the rods moved and we pulled our boat back as far as we could as there was a reserved space behind us. The boat the other side of us did not move and the owners went inside. With my husband and our friends help, the boat squeezed in tightly to the space. Some hours later, we were eating dinner on our deck, and the boat's owner banged on the side of our boat and stuck his head through our canopy.

"You ******* English make me sick, none of you would let me in "

Our friend, tried to calm the situation. The man stood outside, with his bottle in his hand. We explained that there had been a hire boat the other side of us when we moored, and the space was adequate for a small boat, not a 25 m. He complained that he had been moored on the picnic spot further along the river, in front of a campsite, a place we have moored before, and a French man had set his dogs on him, screaming that it was his mooring and he had to leave. The next French man, shouting about his rods, had added to his angst and the gap between our boat and the next one was not big enough. Most spaces aren't and as St Jean relies on business from hire boats stopping for lunch then heading off, if you moved the boat every time someone left, you would move the boat three times a day. He eventually calmed down, and then admitted the real problem, he had just bought the boat, and hired someone to move it for him, he was taking it to London, to make a yoga retreat, not a very holistic approach had been taken. He had bought it very cheap, and there was so many things wrong with it, instead of the skipper taking it to England, he was taking it to get it repaired. After a while he apologised, our friend, who was very good with boats, offered to take a look at it the next morning, and ended up working on it until he couldn't stay there any longer, he had a train ticket to Spain.

Our new spot was infinitely more pleasant than the mooring on the river, despite it being opposite a factory, which burned wood all day and night, my moniker of Mordor, as the lights shown across the canal. On the bright side, at least I could see outside, when I took *Bilbo* out for a night time wee!

Matilda was delighted with our new spot as for the first time since we had left, she could properly roam free. The Husband set up the gang plank, so she could come and go easily, and she settled in so quickly, that to my alarm, she started making inroads with the local wildlife.

First a mouse, a frog, a bird, then one morning, I discovered a rat on the mat. Calling the Husband to come out and remove it, he took *Bilbo* back off the boat while I cleared up the mess. What I didn't see, in my speed to remove the corpse, was that the she had bitten the head off the rat, and as I put the mat down on the clean deck, the head rolled out. After an initial killing spree, she seemed to calm down and became fascinated with the local ducks, then several weeks after we had settled in, she stunned one. Our friends came for dinner, and we had hidden in beneath *Bilbo's* dog basket, it an attempt to allow it to recuperate. When our friends left after dinner, so did the duck.

We soon established an easy routine in St Jean, many people come for the season, and do not venture far and it is easy to understand why. Our mornings started with a walk to Blanquarts marina, stopping at the end of the pontoon, for Susan, the lady in the Broads Cruiser, who had taken a shine to him, to run out and give *Bilbo* his morning biscuit and a cuddle. We would then walk the circuit of St Jean, stopping at the boulangerie or supermarket before returning to the boat for breakfast. Most days people would drop by for a cup of tea, as we were enroute to the two big supermarkets, we achieved little, and enjoyed it immensely.

One of the things I have always loved about St Jean de Losne is the book swap in the centre of the town next to the Mariners Museum. As I am a voracious reader, the first time I visited, my eyes light up. Books organised into genres. Always the mantra of take as many as you want, as when people put their boats up for sale, they invariably deposit a bag of books for distribution, now DVDs have become an addition, and when you are holed up with rain hammering at your windows, a DVD is a welcome treat, which unfortunately, is a regular occurrence boating, even in France.

The book swap takes place twice a week, with an hour before for coffee and cake. I have never joined the throng for coffee, although the cake appealed immensely, and usually just managed to arrive half way through the book swap part of the morning as invariably I had got entangled in some chore and forgot the time.

One week, I had bravely booked a hair appointment at the salon in the same street. I had had a disastrous haircut in Spain that Christmas, which had just about grown out and I wanted it tidying up before we set off South. I had foolishly thought in Spain, that as I had got the hang of telling a French hairdresser what I wanted, I would be able to do the same in

Spanish, with my limited vocabulary of Dog, Donkey, Wine and Carrier Bag. I came out looking like a doll from a 70's horror film.

Having endured some pretty atrocious styles during our time living in France, I could only hope for the best Worst-case scenario I will have to wear a hat.

I parted the hairdressers with a spring in my step, for once it was exactly as I had wished for. I returned two years later, and could have cried, so I guess it was my lucky day.

I hurried to book swap, armed with several of the books I had read over the winter, from the stack I intended on changing before we left, handed the old ones in and walked into my favourite place, the room of books.

To someone, who can walk into a bookshop at any time or order some online, you may not appreciate the delight this room gives me. For years I spent a fortune with Amazon, as the three of us are all great readers. Leaving England was a wrench for many reasons, not least our weekly visits to Waterstones, for The Daughter and I.

As I perused the shelves, my back to the door, I heard a voice

" Does anyone know who wrote Chocolat?"

I muttered" Joanna Harris "

Then I realised I was having a déjà vu. In the same room, two summers before, someone asked the same question, to which I had also replied. The initial conversation, led to the enquirer introducing herself and her friend, the friend then becoming a good friend, Karen who accompanied us from Holland with our boat Jantina to France. They had hung up their French boating gloves and returned to New Zealand for new adventures.

I turned around and it was the same person. We had last seen each other when they headed South in their new boat and we headed to Holland to buy ours. Having found the South not as friendly as the North, possibly because there is an everchanging community of Australians and New Zealanders based in St Jean de Losne every summer, they had just arrived back in town. I was delighted to see her, as our acquaintance had been fleeting as we were both in the midst of boat sales and she invited us aboard for drinks later in the week. We had lots to catch up on, in the two years since we had last met we had both sold our businesses, we were the "Fishy Poms" and they the "Wino's", not for obvious reasons, but their business was in Wine Exportation. Life had changed a lot for us all, and we discovered that we had both been to see the same gite complex up for sale on the Canal du Midi, they had perused it further coming to a dead end. Like us, they were looking for the next thing but unsure what to do. Sadly, they put their boat up for sale and return to New Zealand, where half their family were, giving up on their dream of a property in France when they realised there wasn't any money to be made.

One of the things I love about boating is meeting people with new stories. Boaters are adventurous sorts, some more than others, everyone has a story as to what drew you to what you are doing. Rarely do you spend the evening talking about house prices and school runs. Over the winter, some boaters head back to England to hibernate, and get on with their normal lives for six months catching with family and friends, some head to India, it's cheap and hot, others house sit, discovering new places, making new friends, and those lucky Australians, and New Zealanders, return home for their 'summer'. We had spent most of the winter in Spain, although not hot, we managed to escape the freezing temperatures in France, with the exception of Christmas and New Year, when we were tucked up with our daughter, *Bilbo* and *Matilda*, surrounded by snow.

Although we tend to think we English speakers are all the same, we have different traditions and influences. Spending an evening with Robin and Mike we were treated to home-made guacamole and stories of travelling to the Azures in a sailboat. On our next soiree, they cooked a curry and served banana and coconut and regaled us with more stories of their adventures.

To some this was not unusual, the following evening we had other friends on board and referred to the previous days conversation, to which they replied, "Oh, we know loads of people that have done that" Sailors have a lot more fun than canal cruisers, but then we have more fun than people who stay in their houses and don't go anywhere, know your limitations, it doesn't stop me dreaming of seeing giant tortoises in the Galapagos.

Robin and Mike had the cutest dog, a small fluffy white thing we referred to as *Hairy Harry*. *Bilbo* was quite taken with *Harry* and Robin and Mike would walk *Harry* up to our boat and *Bilbo* would run around outside with him, so when they needed to go by train and collect their car, the natural solution was for him to spend the day and night with us. *Bilbo* was delighted, *Matilda* not so much.

It was bad enough having one dog on board without another one. *Harry* seemed oblivious to the bundle of teeth and claws hissing at him, but we decided that the best solution was to keep the dogs in the wheelhouse and *Matilda* in the lounge, which would be fine if she was a dog, but cats climb.

Harry snuggled up to *Bilbo* for protection, more fool him, and *Matilda* sat staring at them all night. I hardly slept a wink as I was terrified she would attack him. It was a relief to hand him back to his owners in one piece, as delightful a guest he had been. *Bilbo* was a bit miffed as his new walking partner had gone home, an as soon as he left, *Matilda* went outside to kill something, guarding her territory.

A couple of days later, we were out walking and returned to the boat to the burglar alarm ringing out. Our rear deck has a fully enclosed canopy which we have sensors for the alarm set, so that if anyone opens the zip and pokes their head through, it will go off. We always put it on at night, and when we go out as a deterrent. Robin had made a batch of Banana and Walnut muffins for us and walked Harry up to see us, opened the zip to leave them on the table and got the shock of their lives!

As our American friends headed off to more adventures, their six-month stint coming to an end shortly, old friends arrived in St Jean, or nearby. In two weeks, we had to separate phone calls asking for help. Mick with his two dogs, had headed off when the canal opened at the beginning of May, with Richard and his dog Amber. It was Micks first experience of the French canals, but as an old hat at the Uk ones, not a major problem, but it's always nice to travel with companions.

When we arrived at Cusey, a small village in the middle of nowhere, where you had to walk to the top of the hill and stand in front of the statue of 'Our lady' to get mobile reception, the boys had solved the problem. We stopped for a cup of tea and let *Bilbo* have a run about with the dogs. Unfortunately, the beautiful *Amber*, a sort of red haired retriever, lost interest in *Bilbo* fairly rapidly and hopped back on her boat, leaving *Bilbo* to run around with his pals, *Billy* and *Meg*. None of us where taking much notice, then I turned around and realised all the dogs had gone. *Billy* and *Meg* usually come back when called, but *Bilbo* does not, I knew the area well as our last boat *Maranatha*, had its engine blow up and replaced some two years previously and the surrounding areas were all farmland, the problem being that the locals sped through the lanes with no regard for life, of any kind.

After much running about *Meg* and *Billy*, herded *Bilbo* back towards the road and I grabbed him, but in his absence, he had managed to cover himself in cow poo, which we would now have to allow in our car. Leaving Mick and Richard to get ready for the next step of the journey, we returned home, with the windows open and a dog in disgrace.

A few days later, the second call came, luckily, they were a little closer, it was the owners of *Beau*, our old boat, which had also been moored in

Froncles, the port now empty as we had all gone. Both couples had set off together, a rarity in itself as they usually holidayed at separate times with friends, but Deidre had sprained her ankle just before the trip and was incapacitated.

A fuse had gone, and like Mick and Richard, they were in the middle of nowhere, without the spares needed. We called in at the local 'Brico' and I picked up a box of assorted sizes and we headed over there, arriving conveniently, just as they opened a bottle of champagne. We stayed with them for a couple of hours, we hadn't seen Gay and John since they had the news their daughter was getting married, I had seen the photos but it's not the same as talking to the proud parents, now grandparents.

Back to our boat to get on with some repairs of our own. We had received all the fire extinguishers and new cartridges for the life jackets, I had finally got a certificate for our VHF licence, something I had been battling with in Holland, France and finally England to get a licence, Jeff had replaced a piece of tube that the surveyor had recommended the previous owners replace, which hadn't been done and Jeff amazingly, even had time to do some float fishing.

We were ready to leave and go on our way, but our daughter was due to move out in a couple of weeks, so we hung on until she finished University to move her out. Two of our friends had gone to Spain to take their scooter there as they were heading South and would collect it there and we were starting to get bored. The rain hammered down, as is usual in May, we had spent hours watching the Uk election coverage. It was time to move on.

It was the first year we could boat, without having to get back for work and we couldn't leave. Mick and Richard arrived, and Jeff took Richard back to Froncles, I was so bored, instead of a day alone on the boat, I took loads of laundry to the laundrette and sat there with a book.

We went to 'Boat drinks' a weekly get together for boaters in the local area, the first week it was packed as everyone was arriving to their boats, by week three, most people had left, new routes planned. *Beau* arrived in Auxonne, so I invited the two couples over for afternoon tea, forgetting that we were a good walk along the canal and Deidre had a sprained ankle. It was a very odd afternoon. The ladies asked me what I was going to do with the rest of my life? As we had officially been retired for five months, I still hadn't got into that mindset so hadn't got a reply, but as I was in a strange frame of mind, it didn't help. My flippant, I'm on the gap year, that all my friends had when I was working, didn't really cut it, in my mind. We definitely needed to get going, so far, we travelled the same canal we had done at least 4 times and stopped at the same places. I was starting to go stir crazy.

It was also a weird day, as we handed the spare set of keys to them for *Beau*. It had been over five years since they bought *Beau*, but we had always had a set of keys, lest there be a problem. In the winters, when the boat was moored next to us, The Husband had cleared the leaves off the deck, and washed the boat with the Karcher before they arrived so it was clean for them. We checked that the dehumidifier was still working, that there weren't any leaks and when they were there enjoyed many meals aboard, there friends had become ours, it was another door closing, another goodbye.

Our daughter arrived for her last week aboard. We moved the rest of her belonging out of her flat and stuffed whatever we could into our brand-new caravan. I was a little concerned, as the car had become infested with ants, a hazard of being parked near a canal. I couldn't get rid of them, and I was worried that in September, when we went to retrieve everything, the caravan would be teeming with ants, but there was little I could do, apart from pray they all died before September!

It was a strange week for all of us. Our daughter had just waved goodbye to her life in France, she was going to stay with my parents for the summer before commencing her new course at University. Our planned trips with stops for her to visit, were out of the window. We wouldn't see her for three months. It was also my birthday that week and the first not spent at home, friends had sent presents and cards *Poste Restante*, a service in France, where you give someone a post office address and then pay for your post on collection. Some things didn't arrive, the girls behind the counter got sick of me asking if they had any post for me. It was the first time we really felt rootless, it was an odd feeling.

The second problem of not having a French address came to a head as The Daughter moved out, having had all our post redirected to our Uk address, we needed to re-register our car. We had a mooring booked for the winter on the canal Tarn and Garonne at Moissac. Having encountered this problem countless times, Karen, the then manager/Captain of the port, emailed me an Assestation that that was our postal address, a precious piece of paper for us ex pats.

We then had to re-register the French car and caravan at that address, and then Karen had to scan it for us so that we could use the car with the correct paperwork at a later date, it all sounds relatively easy, and it is, if you can read French forms, and fill them in, and you have someone like Karen who wants to help. As we had registered the car before when we moved to a new house, twice, I at least had clue what I was doing, but the uneasy feeling of post wafting around the country with your name on it is not something I enjoy.

My birthday soiree was delightful, Robin and Mike joined the three of us for a bottle of champagne, and spoilt me thoroughly with gifts. The celebration lasted for days as our friend Mick had arrived in town and we decided to attend' boater's drinks' a weekly event at the local bar, and have dinner the following evening. Unfortunately, the heavens opened, and the turnout was low, combined with the fact that the previous week was bumper attendance, buzzing with people eagerly discussing their imminent adventures. Only a smattering of people were present, and Mick arrived an hour later, expecting it to be in full swing, and there was only the three of us and one lady in her Seventies, who The Daughter was enthralled with by her tales, and her gusto. A third attempt at dinner the following evening, on a damp drizzling night, we for enjoyed some local cuisine and The Daughter a last opportunity to put her French to use before she had to think in English again. However, I knew it would be the last Birthday I spent it with The Daughter some years and this saddened me, but it was her choice, we had to let her follow her dream, as we had done ours. A few days later, after lots of people popping in to say goodbye, we drove her to Dijon station to catch the train to Paris to fly to England, to start her new life.

The next day we cast off, and set off on our new adventure.

Chapter Three

New Waters

As someone who spent a lot of time hanging around with carp anglers, as well as being married to one, the term new water, refers to a lake or river, unfished by themselves. We had decided to head to the River Seille, which is a branch off the Saone. For us, this would be new water for boating, but also held the anglers dream, a new unfished area. We had spent some time looking at places to moor on the Saone to fish, but our boat always seemed to be too large, or the spaces were already taken. We didn't need to be in our mooring until November so had plenty of time to get there, a novelty.

Only two days cruising from St Jean, we set off, knowing that once we had travelled a day, we would be on new territory. Our first day took us to an old lock on the Saone, a place we had stopped before in our previous boat. Quite a pretty spot, with a restaurant overlooking the mooring, but even at the end of May, no clients. A lovely place for walking *Bilbo*, and a fascinating house that looked like something from a fairy tale with tiny windows, deserted. It was a relief to be on our way and moving kept me from getting too maudlin about our daughter going back to the Uk.

Our second day, we woke to a dazzling morning and when entered the River Seille it was heavenly. The Husband had made a good call. The Seille is a lesser known river, only used for boating enthusiasts and anglers. At the junctions of the footpaths of the Bresse and the Valley of the Saone, taking it source from the Jura region, it is 112 kilometres long, but only 39 kilometres are navigable. It forms a network of ponds, dunes and peat bogs, sheltering threatened species and migratory birds. For any nature enthusiast, bliss.

Our first night we stopped in a village called La Truchere, not exactly busy, but I am sure chock full in the summer, with an array of restaurants, a speciality frogs, I gather. With a bridge of nine arches and a needle weir, something to see and evidently the fishing was good there too, as a business taking fishing trips on a floating platform, was patrolling up and down, burly men looking like they were auditioning for Bear Grylls. What I enjoyed was the ability to walk back to the lock and stand and watch people coming through, something I don't normally partake in, but when you have a dog you can be nosy. There was also the most beautiful house overlooking the lock entrance, something that you would expect to be a chambre de hote but actually a private house. For the second time, in two days we paid for mooring and topped up with water. It was good to give the batteries a charge as we had not been on mains since we left Froncles, as the power in St Jean was not switched on, our solar panels and generator taking up the slack when we weren't moving. Also filling up with water, we now held enough water to last for a month. The stone benches dotted along the walkways, still wore the sun's vestigial warmth, and we basked in it, enjoying our new environment.

After La Truchere we entered the Seille properly. The novelty of travelling this small river, was that the lock was not automatic, or assisted, you had to do them yourself. We had driven over a few weeks before to have a sneak preview, so I had an idea what to expect when I hopped off. I definitely need to learn to steer the boat, then I would have got out of doing it.

It wasn't a huge problem, as long as you didn't have boats coming in both directions, trying to operate the locks at the same time, still we Brits are good at queueing.

We arrived at our next spot Cuisery, we were far too big for the port, but there appeared to be a mooring spot with one post. After a quick look to check there weren't any signs to say mooring prohibited, I jumped off and got a rope onto the post and Jeff threw me one of ours. It never ceases to amaze me how people think it is a good idea to stand right next to a boat when you are mooring. In this instance, it was necessary for Jeff to throw our sledgehammer onto the grass while I was holding onto the bow rope. A lady decided at this time, to stop by the boat for a chat, and then followed Jeff, over to where he was banging the post in, and no I don't mean a mallet, we really use a sledge hammer, they are big posts, and then hover over him smoking. Apart from the obvious health and safety issues with her being in such close proximity, the cigarette smoke she was blowing over him was making him cough. Not a good start.

Once we got the stakes in, the gang plank was lifted off and he set about cutting back the foliage that was not overhanging our deck. *Matilda* was delighted with her rural surroundings as we had been on a pontoon the two previous nights, and ran over to the woods opposite, in search of some innocent victim, with rushes along the bank she had plenty of cover. After taking *Bilbo* for a quick wee, we retired inside for lunch when we heard a commotion outside the boat. A man was pacing up and down the bank, shouting into his mobile phone. Oh, great we have the village lunatic outside, not a unique experience when boating.

After some time, he switched off his phone and set up some fishing tackle and sat down, getting his black Labrador out of the van and attaching her to the tree adjacent. The Husband decided to go and say hello, it was obvious he was carp fishing and tried to break the ice. Something was lost in translation and he did not receive the desired effect and then he made a second, more successful attempt. By the end of the afternoon, Jeff, and Franck, were chatting away, as best they could.

By late morning, Franck had arrived and was setting up. It seemed that he fished in the same spot every day. By late afternoon he was joined by his girlfriend, Genevieve, a petite brunette in her late twenties, who fortunately, spoke a little English, village lunatic he may be, but it seems we would get to find out, he's our lunatic now.

With the daily talks on carp fishing, Jeff set up his fishing tackle from the bow of the boat, the two anglers egging each other on. Meanwhile, the animals settled into the peaceful environment, surrounded by nature.

Bilbo was taken for walks at six every morning, giving me a rare lie in, The Husband studying the water for areas the fish we are feeding. *Matilda* rarely came home, she found various hiding places when the locals arrived, letting their dogs off the lead for their country walk.

I felt healthy for the first time in weeks, cycling safely every day and getting away from the sociable environment of St Jean de Losne, we had stopped drinking, The Husband swapping his evening glass of wine for a cup of tea on the edge of the boat, and me sitting contentedly beside him. For the first time in many years he was fishing, without anything to prove, purely for enjoyment.

The port at Cuisery had a small marina, overlooked by a restaurant/ snack bar a swimming pool and a campsite. It was an idyllic setting, we were fortunate to get moored there. We had a few boats moored next to us over the time, but the port was busy all the time, the river was used by hire boats heading to Louhans a small market town. We had visited Louhans by car when we were in St Jean after being recommended by some friends, I decided I wanted to visit on my birthday, so we spent the day somewhere new and memorable. It became memorable as we arrived on the day that all the shops closed! The market, which was the big draw for the town and one of the biggest in the region, was on the previous day. So, we arrived on weekly closing, typical. We did take time to walk to the port at Louhans, and established that there wasn't space big enough for our boats, so we opted to stay in Cuisery and retrieve our car from St Jean, using it to investigate the region, with the air con on.

We were intrigued as to why our new fishing friend Franck had so much spare time and discovered he had had an accident at work and was on sick leave, as a lorry driver. We needed to recoup the car and asked if he would drive us to St Jean to get it and we would pay him. As his girlfriend had a day off, he jumped at the chance of a day out and a change of scenery, and spending two hours in the car we certainly got to know a little more of the area and our new friends and their sense of humour.

With our car back, and a renewed enthusiasm in angling, The Husband and I drove to the nearest big town of Macon (and producer of my favourite wine) to a fishing superstore and stocked up on hooks and bait. We had tried to buy some items in Auxonne when we were moored there, but after a needle in a haystack search for the tackle shop, we found it had closed down.

 Both Decathlon, where we had shopped to buy a fishing bed, a copy of the product we had sold worldwide, our patents expired, and Pacific Peche, where we were headed, were both companies that approached us to supply them when we first entered the European market, some fifteen years previously. We had declined the offer and we were reluctant to spend any money with them out of principle, the very products they were selling, the reason we had ducked out of the business and undoubtedly the reason why the little tackle shop had closed. No one can win against these massive companies. Battling with Chinese imports aside, now we were able to actually go fishing and we left the shop guiltily, with rather a lot of purchases.

Being back with nature was all wonderful, but by six every evening nature got us. We were moored with trees adjacent to us and as we settled down for an evening's fishing, the mosquitos settled into us. All the windows in the boat have mosquito panels on the windows, and the door has a separate frame that we use in the summer with a half panel of mosquito net so inside the boat was protected but also thirty-nine degrees, the days were sweltering, and it took until around ten before it was bearable to sit inside, not that we wanted to as we were trying to catch the elusive carp and catfish in the river.

Covered in mosquito repellent, candles ablaze, we were treated to an abundance of wildlife, only disturbed by hire boats chugging along, canoeists, and the odd rowing boat. It was on one such evening, as we basked in the late evening sun, swatting off the occasional insect, that we received an unwanted addition to our household.

As I mentioned previously, *Matilda* was spending little time onboard, only coming in to eat. She had taken to sleeping on the rear deck, and we would often be woken by her running around the boat and then hurtling herself through the bedroom window, onto our heads.

As we started to pack away the tackle for the evening, *Matilda* raced onto the deck and ran through into the boat. What we didn't realise was, she was chasing a mouse, and had kindly invited it into our home! As it was getting dark, we hadn't actually seen the mouse, but it only took a day to be sure it was living amongst us. *Bilbo's* dog chews, had been nibbled. Perhaps the mouse wanted to keep its teeth clean with Denti sticks.

We searched high and low but could not find it. First, we set traps, whilst I removed the contents of my cupboards, threw out anything that may perhaps have been accessed, and drove to the supermarket and bought lots of plastic boxes, transferring everything into them. After a week, we still hadn't located the mouse and we were concerned that it may start munching on the electric cables and cause some real damage. We decided to call in the big guns. We drove to Le Clerc supermarket in Macon and I purchased some sticky pads. These are the most awful inhumane things, although I don't think mouse traps are exactly user friendly.

When we had our lakes, our clients used to bring them and put them in and around their tents to stop mice chomping their bait, I used to complain bitterly and tease them that they were afraid of a little mouse. We caught the mouse, within a day. I let The Husband deal with it as I was so upset we had killed an innocent mouse. I blame *Matilda*, she was supposed to keep them out, not welcome them in.

Mouse gate over, we got back to the all-important task of angling. By the end of the week Franck and his Geneviève had invited us to join them for aperitifs where they were fishing. It was an odd evening, mainly because after an hour, they had to leave for dinner with her mother. I was curious as to whether he would go and change or visit in his fishing clothes.

Franck asked us if we would guard his spot for him on Sunday morning as several of his friends were coming fishing with him and they wanted to fish in his spot. At 7.30 on Sunday morning, I found myself sitting with rods set up in position, lest someone else arrive not from his group, *Bilbo* at my side. They arrived a couple of hours later and set up, happy as all the spaces along the river had been taken.

I was happy to escape into the town and leave the boys to their 'Carp Fever'. A phrase that The Husband had explained it's what we call it in the Uk, a Passion for Angling, and to which Franck called out, with a beaming smile at regular intervals.

Cuisery is one of the four towns in France, with the title, Town of books. As an avid reader, I was most excited when I read this in our boating book before we arrived. The walk into town from the river was up a steep hill but for me, it was worth the trek.

The town of books only consisted of two narrow cobbled streets with book shops flanking either side, but I found it charming. It also housed an original printing press and cafes were dotted in between the shops, slim men dressed in black, smoking and looking intellectual. The first Sunday of every month was a street fair, more books, and music.

The town also contained a record shop, which I had already purchased some CD's for The Husbands birthday, but there were so many that I wanted to buy, I didn't know what to choose. The books I refrained from purchasing, because they were in French, had The Daughter still been living in France, I would have picked some up for her, but having read some translations of French books, when we first moved to France, I was in no rush to read anymore.

Stepping to the end of the street brought you back to reality, a normal French town, which for us luckily had a post office, something that I would find, once again, I would need, for Poste Restante.

Perhaps, a week after we arrived in Cuisery, the temperatures had soared, and we noticed that the charger for our solar panels seemed quite hot. As it was the first summer we had spent on the boat, and also the first year with these solar panels, as the old ones had been taken away and Jeff had replaced with new, more powerful ones. We were unsure if the charger being a tad warm was a normal occurrence. We had used the same panels at our lake, and the same charger so we were familiar with the system and not had any problems, so we put a fan on the charger to cool it down (using more electricity)

This did not solve the problem, and after smelling burning, we realised the cable was melting. We had blown up the charger. It could have been a lot more dangerous that it was, had we been cruising we would have been stuck. We ordered a new charge controller to be delivered to the post office in Cuisery and then we had the fun of trying to buy some cable to replace the frazzled wires we had.

Although France has a lot of sun, solar power is still not that popular, more in the South, but the government stopped subsidies years ago and the incentive has gone. We looked at a house for sale previously, that had a whole room full of batteries in its basement, selling the power back to the grid, but they are rare.

We did know of one set of people that used solar power, other than boaters, although not to the same extent, motorhomers. So, we looked up the nearest motorhome shop and set off, after making sure everything was disconnected! The journey was perhaps an hour away and we found the shop successfully, but it was closed. There was a notice, stating it was closed that morning due to unforeseen circumstances but would be open at 2, it was 2.30! Never one to give up easily, I suggested that we called in at the nearby supermarket for supplies and returned afterwards. I am an eternal optimist, I was sure if we returned it would be open.

Sometime later, the shop was open, many people had obviously had the same opinion and had waited. Unfortunately, the person who had opened up was not a member of the shop staff but one of the admin staff in the motorhome sales department. There were several sales staff if we wanted to buy a new motorhome, but no one that knew anything about the products in the shop.

The Husband was getting agitated, stating we were wasting our time, so I suggested he wait in the car and I would sort it out. Charm and politeness always helps and within minutes, one of the sales team had found one of the mechanics, who had arrived with two reels of solar cable. I then smugly retrieved Jeff from the car, as I was unsure which was the best, as we only expected there to be one variety, and he chose some, muttering that it was going to be very expensive, and returned to the car.

The workshop man, cut the necessary cable and returned to his work, while I queued in the shop. The lady behind the till was flustered as she didn't know how to operate the tills, the shop was still in semi-darkness but a huge queue had formed, it being June, the height of the season. After an interminable amount of time, she made an invoice for me and charged me €16, it should have been about €50. I paid quickly and got in the car, my patience had been rewarded.

The charger arrived a few days later, but not without drama. I had ordered it on Amazon and for some reason the supplier had despatched it without a name, only the post office address, on the day of the delivery, the driver had telephoned me to tell me they were delivering it and I had received an email with the link to show it had been signed for.

I walked up to the Post office, hoping it wasn't too heavy, as it was a long way and I certainly couldn't cycle it and there was nowhere to park. I had already been in every day that week asking the lady, and collecting connectors that we needed for the rewiring, so she knew I was waiting to pick it up.

When I arrived, she told me that a parcel had been delivered, but I hadn't a name on it. It took a lot of pleading for her to hand over the box. Now, if I order anything, I make sure I duplicate my name in the address panel, it could have been a costly error, and also prevented us going on our way.

Despite the enthusiasm of the angling, we didn't seem to be catching many fish. We were doubtful as to the quantity in the water, particularly as this was a region where carp was served on the restaurant menus. Genevieve's father, owned a restaurant along the river in the nearby town of Tournus and she had invited us to join her there but with specialities of Frogs legs or fried carp, we weren't eager to try. I found it hard to understand, how Franck could spend his time trying to catch an elusive carp, when she was serving them up for dinner.

When we had fished on lakes in France, to get bait into a place you can't cast to, it is not unusual to use a bait boat, a remote-control boat that you can send to a precise spot and drop the hook and bait over the top of. The Husband elected to utilise our large plastic boat, kept aboard for emergencies as a makeshift bait boat, rowing the bait across the river.

When we first bought our first lake, *La Fritterie*, he used to do this daily, for two purposes, to distribute the food evenly about the lake, and so that he could catch some of the blighters himself.

It took me back to that time, when the future was ahead of us, and we were filled with hopes and dreams of our new life in France. It was also a time when he lost lots of weight, as he continued doing it when I went back to the Uk. Not something to be discouraged, extra exercise.

After a few days, and some successful angling, under the guise of safety necessity, he suggested we buy a larger boat. The concern was that the boat he had been using was not large enough for two adults, a huge dog and a cat carrier. An advert on the Bon Coin, found a second hand one, and we (I telephoned) and made an appointment to view it.

We arrived at the house, relishing a ride out in the country, taking in the quaint houses in the region. The elderly couple that were selling it had telephoned their son to help, and I presume for a little security, it was something that I had been concerned about when our daughter was clearing out her apartment, letting strangers into your home. The boat was kept at the bottom of their enchanting garden, a combination of flowers and vegetables, a riot of colour and smells. Tucked away in the greenhouse was the boat, exactly what we needed, and we certainly would be noticed if it was in the water, it was bright orange.

After we carried carefully down the garden and strapped it onto the roof of the car, we were invited for a cold drink on the terrace. The house was of similar style to the region we lived in and we spent a pleasant time chatting to them, they were intrigued as to our life on the boat, and as always, what we had been doing in France at all. We said our goodbyes reluctantly, racing back to sit on a hot boat after a shaded veranda was not appealing but we had enjoyed our break away from the boat to civilisation.

Later that evening, The Husband tried out the new boat and it spent the rest of our stay tied up to the side of our barge, ready for action. Our old boat we gave to Franck, I still don't think he had a lot of chance catching a carp or catfish, but he was thrilled at his gift.

The second week we were moored in Cuisery, Franck informed us, he would not be back to fish on Monday and we would not see him until the weekend, he had a new job starting Monday morning. We congratulated him, mainly because I think Genevieve was fed up with him being at home, he was supposed to be decorating her father's house but kept disappearing to fish, we hoped we weren't encouraging him.

Monday afternoon, we were very surprised to have a tap on the door, Franck was back. I asked him why he wasn't at work and he sheepishly told me he had been sent home, he had taken a lorry out and hadn't checked the trailer attached was properly secured, it had veered off and caused an accident. He was adamant it wasn't his fault, and we realised that perhaps he was not particularly good at his chosen career.

With our electrics functioning, and some carp caught it was time to think about leaving. We wanted to get onto the Rhone before the French school holidays started and it became crazy on the waterways but with all the faffing about I still hadn't had the chance to visit Louhans, well, not when anything was open. The advantage of visiting of a 'closed' day for the town was that with few people about we had the opportunity to take in the fabulous architecture. Louhans boasts the longest arcaded street in France with one hundred and fifty-seven arches with over one hundred shops nestling underneath, can you imagine how frustrated I was when they were all closed! It also has a tower and two churches, both with the magnificent coloured tiled roofs common to the region, a treat to view.

Having learnt the hard way that the market was on Monday, early Monday morning we set off for Louhans by car. We arrived at bedlam, parking seemed to be a free for all so The Husband suggested he stop where we were, and I found my way into the centre. I didn't have far to walk before reaching the first row of stalls. I, suppose sometimes I can be a bit silly. We all have different ideas as to a French market, to me it is the type that Rick Stein shows on his television programmes, food stalls overflowing with delicious looking produce. Having lived in a French town for ten years, the first year and whenever we had visitors, I availed myself of the facilities in the market, but had the generally feeling that I was being exploited as I was English, the prices for the fruit and vegetables were extortionate, I often walked away having spent twenty Euros and only seemed to have bought and avocado and a few peppers, so I tended to give markets a miss. What especially irked me was that the produce rarely seemed local, I would try to find the eggs and cheese and discover that they were from a different region. But I suppose they were still French, or so I hoped.

What I had failed to do before we ventured to the great market of France, was to research it on the internet, had I done so, or used my brain, I would have discovered that it was a renowned chicken market. Louhans is in Bresse, and the Bresse Chickens are supposedly the best, a delicacy. This important snippet had slipped my mind, until I was confronted with cage after cage of birds. In Vitry le Francois, where we used to live, often there would be one stall with live chicks and rabbits, visitors always found this charming, but it disturbed me, I knew that the rabbits were not to be kept as pets. Our daughter had pleaded on one occasion for us to have a rabbit as a pet, but we had wild rabbits hopping around the property at our other lakes Orchard and Willow, and red squirrels roaming freely in our woods, badgers and foxes wandering across our lawns, wild boar stampeding in the fiends adjacent and deer jumping over the fences escaping the hunters.so we had no need of buying any, plus we had five kittens at the time.

 As time passed, and we would walk through the market on the way to primary school, passing the stall, the novelty wore off, within a short time she had become 'one of them', rabbit was served weekly on the school menu, rather different to the Turkey Twizzlers Mr Oliver was busy trying to ban, that she had left behind. It wasn't just chickens that were on display, I felt so distressed I bought some goats cheese and eggs and left. I preferred the town, *Sans Marche*.

Our last day in port was rather busy. I drove to Macon and left the car at the port there. There was an international rowing competition taking place, so as I walked along the river and watched everyone getting ready for their big day. I had arranged to take the train to Tournus, the nearest town the train stopped at, and Franck had kindly offered to collect me from the station and drop me back to Cuisery. As arranged, I texted him when the train was at the previous stop and got off at Tournus.

I had given up hope that he was coming, and decided to walk, taxi's even at train stations being a rarity in France. Franck arrived, covered in dust and apologised for being late, he had been called in to help a friend with some plastering. I felt immediately guilty that I had inconvenienced him, and perhaps lost him some money, but he assured me they had finished the job, that was why he was late. We didn't seem to be travelling in the direction that I thought we should be going in and he said that he needed to pop home and get changed out of his dusty overalls.

We pulled up at some gates, and as they clanked behind me, I started to feel a little alarmed, but my fears dissipated when he offered me a coffee and left me on the terrace with his dog. Parked on the drive was a Citroen 2 CV, a car I wanted to buy when I was eighteen, also parked on the other side of the grounds was a Citroen Van. Franck then appeared freshly showered and told me they belonged to Genevieve's brother, who had bought them to restore. The house belonged to her father and they were living there, under the condition that they redecorated it before he moved in. He then proceeded to take me round every room and show me what he had done, or rather what he hadn't.

When he lead me downstairs into the sous sol, a basement running the length of the house, I started to panic. Images of being tied up in the basement came to mind, what was I doing getting into a car with this man, we didn't know him, had I been too trusting, again?

Some years before, we had become friends with a couple and at some stage he become obsessed with me, declaring his love and devotion for me. It brought an abrupt end to our friendship and left me wary of French men in general, the boundaries were blurred, situations they deemed normal, unacceptable.

I was kicking myself for letting down my guard, perhaps this time would be the end of me. As Franck enthusiastically showed me his tackle, he had brought me downstairs as he kept his bait boat and rods down there, I started to relax a little, but I was still nervous. Those feelings will never leave me now, and his behaviour reminded me of Pierre, known after the event, to my friends as The Stalker, which is why it was so unnerving, none of us saw it coming. Although, my mother on meeting him, noticed a couple of things that were a bit odd, but by then it was too late.

So, I found myself looking around the room for an exit, these rooms usually have a side door, we used to have one in our last house. Then, he said he needed to make his lunch and proceeded to demonstrate how to slice shallots and tomatoes finely and make a dressing with olive oil!

We arrived back at the boat sometime later, The Husband concerned as to my whereabouts, perhaps the same thoughts had crossed his mind. I felt I had had a lucky break, and to be warier in the future. Poor Franck was oblivious to my thoughts and set up his fishing tackle for the last day with his funny English neighbours.

By lunchtime, our friends Deidre and Michael had arrived. They were staying on their boat in Auxonne for the week and had gathered together some pastries and bread and telephoned on the way to see if we were free. We set our table and chairs up under the trees and dined on pate, cheese and baguettes, my Billie Holliday Cd, bought at the book fair, wafting across from the boat. Franck joining us for our last day in Cuisery, tomorrow we would re-join the Saone, at set off on the next leg of journey, to join the Mighty Rhone.

Chapter Four

"Sur le Pont"

Leaving Cuisery was a wrench, we were happy in our environment, had made some good friends and spent some time quality time together, caught a few carp and catfish and regained our balance together. However, once we decided we are on the way, then that's it, onwards and upwards. We woke to a perfect Sunday morning in June, the early morning sun dancing across the water and I set off to open the lock for *Jantina* to enter. Unfortunately, I had just finished opening the gates when I hire boat sped in. We are far too big to go into the lock with another, and I was more than a little annoyed that I had walked some distance from the mooring to get the lock prepared, *Jantina* waiting by the entrance to the lock and they had the audacity to steam passed us.

I am sure this sort of thing must happen on the Uk canals regular, where the locks are manually operated, but apart from the occasional boat that has overtaken us on the way into a lock after we have activated it, we have not had any problems. I sat behind the lock and they had the impudence to leave the lock gates open at the other side and race off leaving me with the gates to close and then open the entrance again. I was not a happy bunny.

After the lock, we soon exited the idyllic River Seille to the more hectic River Saone heading towards Macon. We made several unsuccessful attempts to moor. The pontoons belonged to restaurants waiting for their Sunday lunchtime trade, and didn't welcome a boat taking up the same amount of space as four speedboats. Finally, we arrived at a charming mooring on a campsite. It was early afternoon and we were looking forward to a quiet afternoon before the big event.

The pontoon was adjacent to a restaurant and as expected on a Sunday afternoon in June, it was brimming with people, many of whom seemed fascinated by our boat and took it upon themselves to leave their tables and wander down to the pontoon to walk passed the boat and stop outside, asking a stream of questions. I opted to leave The Husband to fend off the enquiries, whilst *Bilbo* and I had a nose around and established where we had to pay.

The campsite appeared a professional operation and had a security barrier with a kiosk. The kiosk also doubled as reception, this was the place to pay. I explained that we were moored up and enquired as to the cost and I was informed I needed to bring ID.

After depositing *Bilbo* back on the boat, I went off to pay, and to my delight I used my recently acquired membership card for the Caravan and Camping Club, something that I had purchased, along with a European Card for us to use in the winter with our Caravan in Spain. I had read online that some campsites ask you to leave your passports for the duration of the stay and by having a European Camping Card this avoided that as it has all the necessary information.

The receptionist scanned the cards, and filled out the paperwork, a lot of rigmarole for one night but after all this is France. She then told me that the electricity was not working now, it would not be switched on until the season started in July! She did comment that the water was switched on and she would only charge me for mooring for the inconvenience of not having electricity. After the transaction was completed, she commented that there was going to be some dancing later, perhaps I might enjoy it. I was a little affronted as I had seen a poster for a Tea Dance, I must be looking rough, how old did she think I was!

We returned to the boat and made use of the facilities by throwing on a load of washing and filling the boat up with water, it had been two weeks since we last had any, so it took a while. After we grabbed something to eat, the tea dance started, and we sat in the shade of the deck, listening to a selection of Swing and Fifties Rock and Roll, which was quite pleasant. By seven, the music had finished, and the cars departed. We had dinner and I took *Bilbo* for a walk around the campsite.

The pontoon was situated at the end of a car park, and I we walked back to get on the boat, I noticed a new set of cars arriving. I assumed that people were arriving for dinner, but they all seemed quite young. As it started to get dark, more and more cars arrived and then music started, not the genteel afternoon music, but banging base. I am not averse to dance music, I was a child of the Eighties and spent the late Eighties/Nineties trawling the country attending raves across the Uk, but that was through choice, and having lived in France for a long time, something I had learnt from many raves thrown on lakes near to ours, the DJ's are dreadful, cannot mix music and it just becomes an awful echoing din.

As the evening drew on, the music got worse, they seemed to be throwing any old record together, Beyoncé and Queen and the base banged on and on. Looking out of the lounge window, I saw several boys swinging off the rafters. The din went on until four in the morning, I suppose we were lucky, it could have been worse. Trying to sleep was impossible, as soon as we drifted off, a change in genre of music would produce a screeching sound from the amps, and wake us from our slumber. Poor *Bilbo* and *Matilda* were terrified, the sound, plus the shouting should have been enough, but the strobe lights flashing through the windows just about topped it.

By five in the morning, the last stragglers left the party, and I took *Bilbo* for a walk then we cast off, bleary eyed and exhausted, our two weeks of rest, destroyed in one night.

We arrived at Belleville sur Saone just after eight in the morning, disturbing the two boats moored up on the pontoon. The first of the two occupants came out, he in his dressing gown and she in her pyjamas to see what all the noise was and then realised it was us. It was our friends Paul and Jennie. The boat moored next to them was our friend Richard with his dog *Amber*, which was good for *Bilbo*, but not so much for *Matilda,* who hopped off, hissed and her and ran up the pontoon into the field opposite.

Once everyone was up and we had had a reviving cup of tea, Richard went off to catch the train to retrieve his car from St Jean, leaving Jennie and I in charge of *Amber*. The two dogs had a great time running up and down the pontoon, as we were the only ones there, there was no one else to annoy.

It had been a month since we had last seen Paul and Jennie, so we had lots to catch up on and after filling my washing machine with their washing, we sat in the sun, with the dogs at our feet. We had seen Richard and *Amber* more recently as they had stopped off at Cuisery for a flying visit on the way to Louhans, his little boat being ideally suited to mooring there, and we had seen him again as he returned. He had left Mick, his then, travelling companion to start a new adventure on the Bourgogne, all the Froncles boats off to pastures new, exactly as it should be, new people to meet and new stories to be shared on our next encounter.

Jeff and Paul decided that we needed to move all the boats round as ours, the heaviest was moored at the end of the pontoon and the wash coming off the gigantic floating hotels, with 200 passengers and crew, were smashing us and the pontoon about. When Richard returned I was on his boat, pulling it round our friends. He had returned reasonably quickly as, is often the way, the train had failed to arrive.

Once we had established that we were staying until the following day, Jennie suggested we had a barbeque, so she and Paul went off into town to get some supplies. *Bilbo* and I went to investigate the area, and decided that as it was, I really couldn't be bothered to walk into the town, I needed to rest after the previous evening. A pleasant afternoon was spent, and Jennie confessed that she really didn't want to go onto the Rhone in their little sail boat, we were mutually discouraging each other, not a good thing.

Late afternoon, we decided to bbq early, it was only at this point that Paul said, have you got a bbq? Jennie had spent ages marinating pork and making skewers up. We did have a bbq, but it was a *Cobb*, which resulted in much ridiculing, as only posers have *Cobbs* apparently.

A Cobb Barbeque is used by boaters as it can sit on the deck of a fibre glass boat without creating any heat or damage. A round barbeque that sits on a well of special 'Cobb Stones' in the centre, like a doughnut in the centre, you can roast vegetables around the outside. The good thing is that it is easy to clean as you swill the well with water and then tip it overboard and the Stones become a solid mass which is bio degradable and you can also pop overboard.

We had one for years, but I hadn't used ours for a couple of years as I am not a great fan of barbeque and really bought it for when we had guests onboard as it was quite expensive to use for two consequently, both it and the magic stones were buried in the bowels of the boat. After pulling lots of stored items out, heaters for the winter, fishing tackle, spare life jackets, I pulled out the Cobb and set it up on the pontoon next to the boat. The idea is, is the stone heats up, turns grey, like normal barbeque coals, and then you pour a little water in the donut part and put the grill part on top. A dome shaped lid accelerates cooking, and keeps the smoke restrained. It seems to take an age to heat up but finally the stone turned grey and I put the first lot of food on. To cook enough food for five would need to be done in rotation but I had made a salad, and fortunately still had lots of goat's cheese left over from last week's trip to Louhans market, so we satisfied with grazing on bread and cheese whilst the meat cooked. Three hours later, the food was barely cooked, I resorted to taking it inside and grilling it. We finally finished eating around ten thirty as it took that long for everything to cook. So much for being a super barbeque, it showed itself to be useless. The annoying thing was, is to clean it, you need for it to cool down and the little grey stone was still burning at 11.30.

As the evening was ending, Jennie and I took *Bilbo* for a walk and decided we needed to find *Matilda*, she had been roaming free since we arrived, not keen to come home as *Amber* was loose on the pontoon. Jennie and I both had flip flops on and the grass in the field was knee high, in the dark we had no idea what was nibbling at our toes, but we felt *Matilda* was teasing us, as we approached her, she would run to another bush. After far too long playing our game of cat and humans, I finally got hold of her and frogmarched her back to the boat. The barbeque was still going, so I threw some water on it and cleaned it out, enough was enough. We had an early start tomorrow, we bade goodnight to our friends, not a time for goodbyes as who knew when we would meet again.

Leaving that morning, I was filled with trepidation, this was it, we were going further than we had ever been, on this stretch of water anyway! We had tried to travel the route a few years previously, with the intention of leaving our last boat *Maranatha in* the South and returning for holidays to cruise when weather and time permitted but a nasty storm felling trees both at home and our lake, had caused us to return to clear up the damage. We had no reason to drag us back this time and no excuse.

We moored along the Saone at Collonge Mont D'Or, not far from Lyon. We still hadn't recovered from our sleep deprivation of Sunday, although we spent the previous day leisurely, we had still had a late night and an early start. We needed our wits about us when we joined the Rhone, so a quiet peaceful spot was just what we wanted. Our intention to get to the other side of Lyon the following day and stay somewhere on the Rhone. I hadn't any great desire to moor in Lyon, neither The Husband or I are big fans of cities and we had driven through Lyon many times on our trips South to Spain. A new harbour had opened but the information stated that we were too large to moor. To our frustration, when we passed it the following day, there were barges moored inside the port, typical, one night would have been nice to have a quick look round.

The pontoon was tucked away on the side of the river, large enough for two big boats with some metal steps leading to the top and a gate. Luckily the gate was unlocked, as we have moored places and you can't get out, not a problem if you don't want to go anywhere, but not so good with a dog that needs a walk. It was a splendid view of the river and a popular spot as there were people 'bivvied up', their tents set up for carp fishing, either side of the pontoon, hidden away in the bushes. There wasn't much of a walk possibly, as it was situated on a main road into Lyon, so I wandered up and down the same stretch, trying to tire *Bilbo* out. Across the road from the entrance to the mooring was a restaurant of Chinese style, with pagodas, but upon investigation it wasn't a Chinese restaurant, it sold typical French Cuisine, disappointing, I quite fancied a Kung Po Chicken!

Parked up in front of the restaurant was a truck loaded with 2 CV's, the second time in a week I had come upon some. I have no idea why they were there but there was also a collection in the car park, so perhaps some sort of meeting, or sales summit, but in the morning, all evidence of them had all gone. Odd.

After I returned from my dog walk, The Husband put a large padlock and chain round the entrance to the pontoon, there had been a number of people come down onto it to wander about. I felt a lot safer knowing that no none could get to us whilst we were sleeping, we were on the outskirts of one of the larger cities in France, and in quite a secluded spot, we could have been robbed or murdered and no one would have known.

Rising early, refreshed and revived, or driven by adrenalin to get through this part of the journey, we made the journey to Lyon in good time. Lyon is the second largest city in France and we expected it to be hectic, yet we have not travelled around Paris, so we really didn't know what to expect. The cities around The Netherlands are much calmer to travel in, despite the huge ships travelling as the people operate the waterways run it in a professional manner. We would soon find out, the same couldn't be said for the lock keepers controlling the vast locks on the Rhone, comedians would be a polite way of describing them. There are other words that we bandied about over the next few days, but I am too polite to use them, on paper anyway.

Travelling through Lyon was fascinating, everything takes a different view from the water, usually with a city, you tend to see the worst as you travel through it, the vagrants sleeping rough, the high rises and graffiti, the hidden ugliness but with Lyon it was an absolute delight. I regretted our decision not to stop, the city was magnificent, I am very pleased I wasn't steering with the captivating old architecture as we approached the city, vying for attention with modern stark architecture, giant squares of red and lime green flanking the new port, and new area as we exited.

Travelling at different times of the year, not only do you get the benefit of the change of the season, but you also get the opportunity to see France for the French, whether it is being fortunate enough to arrive in a town or village during a fete, or come upon a brocante or a musical recital, the activities are not for the benefits of the tourists but for the French themselves that live there. Having lived in a French town, it was lucky enough to be privy to the local events, whether it was being invited to attend the World Ladies Day, which some friends of mine where exhibiting in, or attending the yearly Flower Fete, which friends were running.

Our first year, I was very excited when a flyer arrived in the post box for *Une place de Soleil*, two monthly programmes of events for youngsters. Having packed The Daughter, off to a private school every day for sports activities when we lived in the UK, I had been wondering what exactly I was going to do with her all day, until the English schools broke up. Then we would have our onslaught of English friends staying with their children to keep her occupied as most of her French friends seemed to be going off to their grand-parents for the summer, parents to join as and when. It seemed that as was the norm, only the affluent families were off on holiday, although the government did subsidise French families by giving them vouchers to use at holiday parks across France, making it more affordable, and holding them in the country, instead of wasting their coffers in Spain or Italy, thus keeping the wealth in the country, not a bad idea really.

A few days before the school holidays began, the square in our town was turned into a playground, one year a temporary beach with sun loungers, another year mazes, bouncy castles, uni cycles. Combined with this were shows, mainly at weekends, designed to attract business to the town. Over the years we saw, puppet shows, trapeze artists, the odd outdoor cinema show in the Hotel de Ville Gardens and many singers performing, all free. This wasn't just our town, but throughout France, on a visit to Chaumont on one of our boats, my friend and I took her sons to town to avail ourselves of the facilities. On a visit to Paris, we had seen the banks of the Seine turned into a beach, an on our trip through Lyon, we saw stone sun loungers, not very comfortable, but people were making the most of them, basking in the morning sun. I suppose they were stone so that they weren't stolen, it was a sight to see, and most unexpected.

Exiting central Lyon, passing hotel barge after hotel barge, we now found ourselves approaching the first lock, donning our obligatory orange life vests. I had tuned the VHF radio into the correct station so that we could listen in to any announcements, we weren't newbies at this, we had done it in Holland, but we were still nervous, the advantage being here is that I understood French whereas in Holland we had struggled as our boat was flying the Dutch flag, so naturally, thy assumed we spoke Dutch.

The Edouard-Herriot Commercial Port in Lyon is part of a huge transport system where water transport is linked to road and rail handling more than 10 million tonnes of merchandise, of which 1.2 million by barge, servicing as a terminus between Lyon and Marseille, not surprising there was a lot of traffic, it was the boating equivalent of the M25 .Trip boats carrying passengers were passing in, commercial vessels and small boats all seemed to be trying to get into the lock at the same time, and no one was telling us what to do, I had announced our arrival and we were told to wait for the day trip boat to come through, not a problem had there been anywhere to moor but the waiting pontoon was already occupied, by a work boat, something that we later discovered was not unusual. This left us waiting mid water until we were instructed we could enter the lock, we had expected a wait of perhaps forty-five minutes, as to save water they must put through as many boats together. What had not been explained to us was that the boat was going through the lock, turning around and coming back through again towards us, doubtless to drop off the passengers and then pick up the next group. The lock was not full up, we easily could have fitted in as well, we waited patiently then entered when the lock light changed to green, the lock was 9 metres high, the locks on the Saone, 3 metres, a big contrast. Inset in the walls of the lock were floating bollards, once we worked out how best to attach the ropes it wasn't a problem, we had experience of them in Holland, but It was eighteen months since we had been in one and with noise and chaos around you it is difficult to concentrate, the biggest fear that the bollard stuck and stopped floating, which would cause the rope to snag and either the rope would break, or the boat would hang onto the side of the lock. We had had a rope jam, on one of the first locks we entered in France, when we brought *Jantina* from Holland, our first tiny lock causing us more trouble than the gigantic locks in The Netherlands and Belgium. In five years of boating we had never had a rope snag, but had always kept a sharp knife to hand. When we bought *Jantina*, we had purchased some garden shears from the local garden centre, our barge ropes were 18 plies, they needed something a bit sturdier than a kitchen knife. When we had to cut the rope in that lock we were cross with ourselves, especially as our new ropes were rather expensive and you don't have time to make a cut to keep half the rope intact.

For this lock the Pierre Benite, we had our shears out on the deck ready for action. As we exited, and I thanked the lock keeper on the VHF, I breathed a sigh of relief, I actually found the big lock easier than the little ones. The same couldn't be said for Jeff, mumbling about it being ridiculous that you couldn't tie up with waits for up to an hour. I hoped the next lock would be less stressful, after all it was the first lock, deep in the industrial area, on the outskirts of a vast city, they couldn't all be as bad as that, surely. While he was getting used to being overtaken by push tugs. Carrying 4,400 tonnes of cargo, I was providing an annoying commentary on our surroundings.

In 1967 The Pierre- Benite barrage was constructed, by La Compagnie National du Rhone, installing small hydroelectric power station. We were now travelling under the jurisdiction of the CNR, not VNF and through a website that our friends had given us the link to, we were able to study readings of the flow at each of the locks to help us make decisions along the way. I found this fascinating. the CNR manages 33 power stations for an annual production of 16 billon kilowatts per hours, which is sadly still only 4% of the national production, but it was great to find out that they were also setting up projects for wind farms further South, towards the end of the Rhone. We would catch sight of the hydroelectric power station at Bollene, in a few days when we had the fortune, or misfortune, depending on your view, of entering the largest lock in Europe at 22 metres 50 deep, perhaps not as easy as this one.

I soon established that cruising along the Rhone was going to require a little more effort from me. Usually, if we are travelling a period without any locks, I will go into the galley, make lunch, do some cleaning and then sit in the wheelhouse and read, or chat to The Husband. It seemed that I would spend my time alternating with looking behind to check nothing was overtaking, and standing on my tip toes, trying to read the information transmitted on our AIS, a system which identifies boats on the water (if they have the system).

At the time it was not necessary, but was coming into force, that boats over twenty metres, which ours was, would need this piece of equipment. Sail boats tended to have it, the same as the VHF Radio transmitters, as they use more perilous waters and it allows coastguards to identify the whereabouts of the boat by its number and coordinates being transmitted. On this particular journey, we were able to identify if large vessels where approaching, from what direction and at what speed, my job was to tell The Husband, what was coming, and how quickly. It was particular useful when approaching bends, bridges and locks as you could adjust the speed accordingly, hanging back where necessary. We had experience of this before, but the sheer volume of traffic using the waterways was terrifying, well I was terrified anyway.

We approached the next lock Vaugris, not quite as high, at 6.7 metres and the lights were on green so we sped up, as we got close to the lock, the lock lights were changed to red. I had already announced our arrival to the lock keeper, who told us to enter the lock, so we were perplexed when it the lock lights were changed to red. I quick look round and The Husband reversed to the pontoon to moor up. The waiting pontoons feature two dolphins, large concrete posts with metal bars on them, and a pontoon in the centre. At 20 plus metres, manoeuvring into the pontoon meant passing the first dolphin then swinging into the pontoon. Easier said than done.

One of the many reasons stories are exchanged about a Rhone expedition, is the wind. The Rhone has a current that can exceed 12kph, combined with The Mistral, a northern wind which can blow any time of the year and is extremely strong. Not being a boating person, prior to the purchase of our first boat some seven years earlier, or having a good grasp of Geography, the only reason I remembered the name The Mistral, was because of a book by Judith Krantz, which was made into an 80's mini-series, starring the glamorous Stephanie Powers and Stacey Keach, it had nothing to do with the wind but did evoke powerful romantic images of France. My actual experience of the Mistral was having lunch in Avignon with The Daughter and The Husband a few years ago and the wind being so strong that the tablecloth on the table next to us blew off, along with the glasses and cutlery. There is also a South Easterly wind, it is called the Sirocco, but I'll call it Norma, it sounds like a favourite aunt but, Norma, is less ferocious than her Northern counterpart, but can create a nasty chop. It seemed that Norma and Mistral were playing with us that day, tossing us around like dog with a chew toy, and as we approached the pontoon we careered into the dolphin taking a chunk out of the side of our bow. We got a line on and tied up, but The Husband was not a happy bunny, had we entered the lock initially, we would have avoided this, the fact that we had reversed backwards with wind buffeting us about caused us to be in a bad position, plus the knowledge that something was steaming up behind us, which we would then have to wait to enter added to the pressure to get out of the way and moored. As soon as we got the stern rope on, the lights changed to green, it appeared it wasn't just the wind that was playing with us.

It was now early afternoon, we had intended on mooring in the ancient town of Vienne, but the town walls were full, hardly surprising as it was June, but you can live in hope, we carried on to the next stop we had marked off. The Husband had been studying various sites with info and had marked off possible moorings on the map. I am continuously frustrated when we pass a lovely looking mooring in a town, on a river there is no possibility of stopping unless there is a designated mooring, at least on a canal, on our boat, we can stop and put pins in, where it allows.

The port of les Roches de Condrieu was our next choice, just outside the town of Condrieu, where white wine is made, the grapes originally brought to the Rhone valley by the Greeks. Alas, we were not going to have the opportunity to taste any, as the port at Condrieu was for little boats.

We continued along and shortly found ourselves at a small pontoon at a place called Chavanay. There was a notice on the dolphin that mooring was prohibited at certain times, fortunately, it was not one of those times. I sometimes think that if Lisa the Linguistic hadn't ever learnt any French we would have been stuck, as it was not the first time we came across notices like this and without understanding the nuances, we may have carried on, to who knows where, or stayed until we got shouted at, depending on our mood and level of fatigue.

The pontoon was perfect, *Matilda* was able to come outside and wander up and down, finally settling in a sunny spot for a snooze. At the top of the pontoon was a cycle track and walks into the village, *Bilbo* and I both, were glad to get away from the river and have somewhere to walk where juggernauts weren't hammering passed us, also the ramp leading to the exit gate was in, what I call nasty spiky metal, something that is used regularly on the pontoons and were as unpleasant on the soles of my *Skechers* as *Bilbo's* feet. Jeff took one our carpet runner from the lounge and lay it along the ramp, so Bilbo could walk up and down without hurting his paws, then carried *Matilda* up to the top so that she could go for a wander and walk back herself, he is a softie really.

As we had bumped the boat, he decided to do some temporary maintenance, rust treating and repainted the offending area. Our friends Robin and Mike, had told us that when we had 'done 'the Canal du Midi we would need to repaint the boat, we hadn't even done the first leg of the trip. I fear there will be lots of touching up during this journey. At the top of the mooring was the remains of some 14th Century fortifications, that would do me for sightseeing for the day, a quick walk around the village's winding streets over a bridge with *Bilbo*, was enough for me. There had been a suspension bridge built in the 19th Century across the Rhone, but the bridge had disappeared, leaving the old pylons near the mooring point. I was quite content to sit on the boat and watch the lunatics crashing around on their speed boats as they left the port, which we were unable to moor in. I think we had the better deal, happy pets and happy husband, what more could you ask for.

Later that evening, energy levels replenished, The Husband got busy and decided to take our newly purchased boat and place it on the rear deck, not without some assistance from me as it was much heavier than the old one. It was a déjà vu of our time at the lakes. In the winter, we used to keep a similar sized boat, in our lodge, green not bright orange, it would have scared the fish! it was one of my least favourite jobs as we had to carry it through double patio doors onto the terrace and then drag it down the bank to the mouth of the lake, we would then carry a battery and small electric motor down to the bank. It was necessary to 'wire up' with cables criss crossed the lake to stop people stealing our expensive livestock and was an arduous task, we often got people to help but would start it off ourselves, as soon as the last client left. When the words, we need to get the boat out 'were uttered, I would always groan, knowing that my back and wrists would ache for the next week. I know realised that we had managed to purchase something equally as cumbersome, requiring us to carry the boat over our heads along the gunnels to the other end of the boat, we tried winching it on and off but then that required us dismantling the outside awning, so it was easier to carry it.

After we had the boat in position, we filled it with emergency equipment, life jackets, the cat box, a spare lead for *Bilbo*, a first aid kit, a battery and the outboard motor, although, quite how we were going to get it all off if we had to go overboard I do not know. It took this lightly, and a manifestation of The Husbands concerns for the trip. When he suggested I make an emergency bag then I started to fear the trip myself. Gathering together some basic items of identify and bank cards, spare glasses and meds, pet passports a spare mobile phone and kept that bag next to the bed throughout the journey, until we re-joined the safety of a canal, taking into the wheelhouse every morning. I am sure it we had a problem, I would have probably lost it in the panic, but it reassured me that I was prepared.

Our Daughter was now living with my parents whilst waiting to commence University, and I tried to keep our progress updated on Facebook as she was working in a hotel restaurant for the summer, so her hours did not necessarily tie up with ours. When I posted a photo of the 'Evacuation boat' and informed my mother that I had just put a bag together in case we had to make a sharp exit, she then realised that this was not a gentle little trip along our local canal, it was potentially dangerous but I endeavoured to appear un phased, telling her it was a great adventure, although inwardly wishing we could get to the Canal Rhone Sete to safety, and wild ponies, much more my thing than the industrial landscape of the first day on the Rhone.

As I had found little time to catch up with any jobs, I decided to dig out my slow cooker and prepare a chilli for the next day, it could cook as we were travelling, and dinner would be ready when we stopped. We anticipated a reasonable day as we had a reservation in the marina in Valence, but we had driven to Valence previously and it was quite a way from the town, so I envisaged us arriving then pottering around the marina, hopefully having a chat with some fellow boaters as we had only had each other to speak to since we left Belleville sur Saone, and perhaps discuss a shared experience or two, to alleviate the tension of the trip. Valence had always been a point on our journeys by car to Spain, when we perhaps saw the sun for the first time, and not so cheerfully, when returning in January or February, the last for some time. When we had stopped off at the harbour, on one such trip, an opportunity to walk *Bilbo*, stretch our legs and suss out mooring for the future, as we pulled into the car park of this large marina, we were greeted by two ladies soliciting. To say it was a bit of a shock was an understatement, which this image in my mind, I had no intention of wandering about without The Husband, not that I thought anyone would approach me in my boaters closed. It was our first impression of the differences between the North and South or France. I once saw two girls standing at the roundabout of the entrance to the town we lived in and naively commented to The Daughter that I had seen the older sisters of a girl on her class at college, who was a gypsy.

The Daughters replied,*" oh yeah, they are both on the game."*

I was aghast, I suppose we all imagine these things don't go on where we live, but it certainly wouldn't have been going on in February, it was far too cold to be hanging about flashing your knickers! On subsequent visits to the South boat hunting it became a sad but regular sight to see girls sitting on a plastic chair in a layby, waiting for their next client, but you don't see these things by boat and sometimes it's better to be unaware of the seedy underbelly of society, as the saying goes, what you don't know, don't hurt you.

We were not going to see, or otherwise, if this was a common occurrence at Valence, as after advancing through 3 locks, of 11 metres plus, we approached the port at Valance and were told we couldn't moor there. I had telephoned ahead to ask which pontoon we were to moor on, and the harbour master asked us how much we weighed, when I told him, he said we were too heavy. So much for our reservation. 3 giant locks with equally challenging mooring pontoons and wind combinations had left us frazzled, we were ready to stop, and usually we would at least stop so that *Bilbo* could have a quick wee, and The Husband, as I was far too terrified to take the wheel (well joystick, one of the things I couldn't master, the precise movement required to control our vessel. Alas, every pontoon we would now approach was full, despite noticing stating that they were purely for waiting to enter the lock and that permanent mooring was prohibited. In the meantime, I got camera happy and took photo after photo of the wine growing region of Crozes Hermitage, and Tain Hermitage, world famous names, at the expensive end of the wine sections we certainly weren't going to be mooring there, as it was reserved for the big cruise ships, spilling their passengers onto the quay, for organised wine tasting and gastronomical delights.

The day seemed to go on forever. Another lock and we attempted to moor on a high wall, The Husband felt it wasn't wise, but I was so desperate to stop. The town had two moorings, one it was obvious that only passenger boats could use as it was so high, the second, still looked too high, but we had moored in Liege a few years earlier in the port and had put the gang plank on the roof and lifted *Bilbo* up. It had taken four of us to do it, as we were travelling with our friends Bruce and Karen, who were kindly helping us bring the boat back from Holland, when we had just bought it. I was determined we would stop as it was now 4 in the afternoon but as we approached the wall, it appeared that the only way to get a rope on was for me to climb up the wall and stand on the top. Bearing in mind that the wall was on the River Rhone, and should I fall there was nothing stopping me falling in and being swept away by the current it wasn't wise, but I tried grappling my way up the wall, much to the protestations of The Husband, it was then that he spied a passenger boat, tearing towards us and hollered for me to get back down, as I would end up in the drink if it passed us. I scrambled back down, and we have up and left, it was impossible to tie up there, unless perhaps you were on a very high cruiser and could stand on the roof to throw a rope, but for our low barge, it was no good.

Two more locks and we still hadn't found anywhere to moor, I made lots of notes of on map, should we ever be insane enough to repeat this journey in a different boat and texted our friends Paul and Jennie, as they and Richard with *Amber* were following us a day behind, and there were lots of lovely moorings for their small boats, taking into consideration good spots for dogs, just not our beast, or if there were they were occupied by other similar sized boats. We approached the lock of Châteauneuf du Rhone at eight thirty that evening, I remembered it as I was convinced that it was where my once favourite wine Châteauneuf du Pape came from. It wasn't, Châteauneuf du Pape was in this region, but further along the river, and of course, the mooring was only for passenger boats. I don't fancy being stuck on a boat with 200 over people for a week but evidently you get to go to places that us mere mortals don't. But then they don't have so much fun on their journey, looking afar from their luxury cabins. I say once favourite for Châteauneuf du Pape, as once you have lived in France, you find that what is sold to England is good, but there are lots more, just as good, and when you are on a boat, you are in the lucky position to try the regional wines, the problem is, I tend to think that I have been to places, when actually I may have just drunk the wine and vice versa, I have been known to buy wine, just because we have visited the region. One such wine, is from the area near Narbonne, in the South, the wine growing region is La Clape, so amused was I to order a bottle of La Clape from the restaurant menu, I spent the evening tittering like a school girl. It was exceptionally good wine and the next day The Husband and I drove to said area and saw all the vineyards, there is something very satisfying from doing that, I can stand in a supermarket, and know where the wine comes from now, and look for brands, as opposed to buying one two bottles for Ten pounds at the Co-op in our village, and not caring what it tasted like!

By the time we had exited the lock at Châteauneuf, which took forever as it was 16 metres 50 high, almost twice the first one on the Rhone, it was dark. We tied up on the waiting pontoon, between the two dolphins, and I contacted the lock keeper on the VHF Radio and asked him if we could stay on the pontoon, it was now nine thirty, we had cruised for thirteen hours continuously. He agreed, with promise that we would leave by Seven the following morning. My first priority was to take my poor desperate dog for a wee, I walked up to the top of the steps, leading to a green wooded area and it was delightful and heavily lit. Returning to the boat, we eat our chilli, stunned into silence, thoroughly exhausted. When we had finished eating, I decided to take *Bilbo* for a good walk, it was a glorious June evening. The Husband decided that as it looked relatively safe, he would carry *Matilda* up the stairs so that she could roll around on the grass. She had spent the day dozing on the bed, oblivious to our plight. We had a pleasant stroll and returned to seek *Matilda* out, but we couldn't find her. *Bilbo* and I walked up and down, looking under bushes, behind trees, she was nowhere to be seen. Just as we got to the point where I was blaming Jeff for suggesting we let her out we heard a faint meow. Using *Bilbo's* tracker dog skills, he eventually located her. The pontoon had two sets of steps arising from it, one of them was for the commercial craft and was locked, our access was further along the pontoon, she had attempted to return to the boat, but disorientated, and hopped down the wrong steps and was sitting in the middle of the commercial steps. The Husband had to climb over the gate and walk down to her, grab her, as she is inclined to bolt, and carry her back up the steps to hand her over the gate to me. With our little drama for the night over, we retired to bed and set off at six thirty the following morning, for another day of fun and games.

So, this was it, today we would enter the biggest lock in the European network, at 22. Metres 50 the matriarch of locks, much photographed by fellow boaters. Ironically, after the previous days exploits, we were actually able to stop at the mooring pontoon, so I took *Bilbo* for a quick wee, while we waited for the boat to come through from the other side. This gave us both the opportunity to look at the Andre Blondel power station, the most powerful hydroelectric station on the Rhone. With only one big lock on the Rhone to go before we reached Avignon, Bollene was our Everest and once over it would be plain sailing, or so we hoped.

Bollene was not as daunting as we expected once the lock started but entering was a cross between a theme park ride and a nightmare. As we entered the lock, announcements were made in various languages over loud speakers, flashing lights and buzzers were sounding, there was a cacophony of noise, it was rather bewildering. A smaller boat behind us had not tied up correctly and one of the lock employees walked along the lock wall and barked at the owners, they had tied a rope onto one of the ladders, which is strictly prohibited, I believe the owners were German and didn't understand, or certainly feigned understanding. Eventually, I called to them in English and told the owners that the CNF worker was telling them to move the rope, he would not operate the lock until they were properly attached. The sheer size of the lock became apparent when the gates banged closed, then the buzzers started to indicate the lock commencing operation. I breathed a sigh of relief, we were underway, and in about forty-five minutes, we would be exiting.

So, the part of the week that I had been worried about was over, one more lock and we would be soon approaching the walled town of Avignon. We had passed almost 200 kilometres of water with the Cotes du Rhone vineyards lining either side of the river, now they were fading into the horizon, the Ile Piot was within our sight. We had no intention of visiting Avignon, as we had taken a trip to the nearby Arles some years earlier and explored the region, spending a day in Avignon. We had visited the sights is a much quieter period, one of the advantages of living in France and being able to go off on a whim to visit places we had heard of as children. It seemed that yet again, we would not stop where we had chosen, as the Mistral and her naughty sister, Norma, decided to toss us about so violently that we were blown across the river. Jeff decided to slow down as we left the main channel and enter the old arm of the

Rhone to try and approach the harbour at Avignon which required a two-kilometre journey up to the Arms of Avignon then an abrupt turn. The wind was underneath the canopy, pulling it away from its fastenings, one of the chair cushions blew off into the drink, and the blue board, a sign we are obligated to have as we are over twenty metres, to indicate to ships if we are not following the usual course, started to bang up and down on the roof. I ran outside, holding onto the rails on the side of the boat and tried to grab hold of it, securing it with a cable tie temporarily. Anything that looked like it would blow away, I grabbed and threw inside, by the time I had completed this, I was crawling on my hands and knees across the deck and the wind was so strong I couldn't keep on my feet, in the midst of all this chaos, the wind had blown open the door into the wheelhouse and *Matilda*, sensing we had slowed down, decided to take a stroll onto the deck, I lunged for her, fell over and grabbed her, nearly squashing her and crawled on my knees back to the door and put her inside, before I secured it and we lost more things not secured. It was the first time during the journey I felt genuinely in peril. We are not sailors, so we are not experienced in strong winds, I can only imagine how terrifying it must be to be in a small boat, when I was so petrified in our heavy one.

The harbour at Avignon is situation in the centre of the city, mooring was alongside a long wall, boats were arriving at a great rate, desperate to stop and get to safety. The lower part of the wall was full of sailboats, where normally we would have tried to moor, there were a couple of spaces along the higher part of the wall, so we had to make do with that. We were too long and clearly too heavy to moor on the finger pontoons that friends of ours had been lucky enough to moor on. After struggling to get the ropes onto the wall, we were tied up, it was Friday afternoon, it looked like we would be spending the weekend in Avignon and yes, we could see the bridge, from the song, although most of it has disintegrated, rather disappointing but at least some of it remains. Avignon is known by some as 'the tower of violent winds' and I can confirm, it is very apt.

If mooring had proved difficulty, getting *Bilbo* off the boat was a nightmare. We resorted to the tactics we had last used in Liege, lifting the gang plank onto the roof and lifting *Bilbo* onto the roof also. This meant that I couldn't take him for a casual walk when the fancy took me, as we couldn't leave the gang plank out as speed boats were tearing around the harbour, resulting in the boat bouncing up and down for the wash and the gang plank banging on the roof. When I did get him off, there wasn't anywhere to walk him as further along from where we were moored was a lane with boats permanently moored. As we attempted to walk along there, the residents scowled at me as their dogs, which were loose outside their boats and didn't appreciate my big baby walking around the territory. As the mooring was adjacent to the ring road through central Avignon, there was nowhere else to go, expect walk up and down the harbour wall on day two I braved it further, but it wasn't a pleasant walk, and I couldn't wait to get on our way.

Avignon is steeped in history, its biggest attraction a fourteenth century Papal Palace, known as the Palace des Papes. It is perfectly preserved and the largest Gothic Palace in Europe. It is pretty understandable that on a Saturday in June the river town would be knee deep in tourists. Friday evening, I had battled the wind and walked to the local Carrefour Market, buying far too much to carry, the selection of fresh produce sending me into a frenzy as the supermarket at Cuisery, where we had stayed for a while, was quite basic. As you would expect in a city, the selection was a little more sophisticated and I was delighted to pick up some yummy food but not so pleased when I exited the shop and remembered I had to walk all the way back through the main shopping street to get back to the harbour, also forgetting that when I did return I had to climb onto the roof of the boat to get on. Taking in the surroundings, I promised myself to return the following morning and perhaps investigate places that I had missed with The Husband and a disgruntled teenager, today I was just happy to get some cherry tomatoes and hummus.

Friday evening, we dined on the deck, taking in the dramatic surroundings, a restaurant was situated across the river, picture perfect, with a selection of singers of different genres, I felt like we were on a film set, this was the life. Lovers strolled hand in hand along the wharf, tourists in droves, taking photos of the bridge, the restaurant and the sail boats moored off shore, bobbing in the choppy water. It was absolutely what we expect France to be like, until our tranquillity was spoiled by a 'disco boat' coming past to turn around at the end of the harbour, rocking the boat and the wine. When it returned an hour later, we decided to go inside, it seemed that the boat would repeat the circuit throughout the evening.

Saturday morning, I ventured back into Avignon, I was on determined, I must find the post office as I had a French tax return to post, my hapless accountant had obviously decided that since I had closed the company down, I didn't need his services to complete our tax return. When he did decide to complete it, then he emailed me someone else's, then when I pointed out this error, he asked me to send him the figures again, of the company he had closed down the previous December, I was beginning to pull my hair out, we had set sail, supposedly free, everything was supposed to be dealt with. When he finally sent me a completed form with our names on, he had omitted our daughter on the entry. In France, your tax liability is calculated on a number of parts, and as a family, so a couple are two, a couple with 1 child is 2.5, this is then divided into your tax liability. Until the age of twenty-five you are responsible for your children in France, and as such, they are part of your tax return. So, he had increased our tax liability by forgetting that our daughter existed, I am not really sure how, as they had been doing our tax since we moved to France, and she used to come to the meetings, particular as she was studying economics in France, it was valuable experience for her. A consequence of the repeated mistakes was that I a little stressed, as I had less than a week to get our tax return to the correct office, I must find a post office somewhere in Avignon, before we set of again, goodness knows where.

My search brought me to the tourist information office. The Captainaire had been closed since we arrived, otherwise I would have asked him/her, and it was a big city to wander around aimlessly, especially as the wind was still so strong, I was struggling to walk. As you would expect, it was a huge tourist office and busy. Many different nationalities were buzzing inside, perusing leaflets and queuing with enquiries. Armed with a map of the town, I soon for the post office, opposite the train station, I felt the burden lift from my shoulders as I posted the envelope. Now I could look at leisure at the magnificent buildings. Walking through the historical quarter, I felt like a tourist for the first time in an age, the narrow winding streets, with shops spilling out their wares, dotted in-between an art gallery or library. I always like to wander off the beaten track and feel that I have seen the guts of the city, usually I will walk the back streets of the town with my faithful companion.at my heels, picking up a croissant on the way. I like to the streets devoid of people, wet from their recent cleaning, the puddles under the flower displays as the gardeners fill their thirsty troughs. The silent streets before the dirt of the day arrives. I had missed the chance to wander Avignon in this fashion as the road was too hazardous to take *Bilbo* across and even at an early hour, the city was hectic full of activity.

As with many towns in France, the heart is usually a square flagged by glorious looking restaurants. Avignon did not disappoint, and to add to the ambience, on Saturday the artists were set up, selling their wares. I approached one, selling various sized oil paintings of poppies. At the time, my mother had a glorious painting of poppies in her kitchen and I had been purchasing her French dishes from the homewares store in the town we lived in over the years, mainly because, whenever I went in, the lady would accost me to look at something else in the range that was in stock, knowing I was an easy touch, and also that I loved presenting my mother with a beautifully packaged gift, something that I haven't ever had the skill or patience to master.

Not one of the paintings were priced up, which is always a worry, and putting on my best accent, I knew it was likely they would double the price when she realised I was English. When I did get a price, I walked away quickly, I was English, not stupid. As it happens, my mother updated the interior of her kitchen, her beautiful poppy painting has been reassigned to duty in the hall, and her French china to the cupboard, it seemed her love affair with France was over now she didn't visit regularly, she changed her décor to Spanish influences, her current vacating place of choice.

On my way back, I took what I thought was a short cut, but my terrible sense of direction lead me in the opposite direction and I ended up walking the walls of Avignon. Somehow, I became sheep like and started following others, to the wrong place. I found myself in a small square, in front of yet another church, to my amusement as I turned a corner, I heard a French voice booming over a loud speaker, an Aerobicsathon was taking place. Perhaps one hundred people were gathered in their lycra, all jumping up and down, with a throng of spectators and bewildered tourists stopping, like myself to see what the commotion was for. I stood transfixed by the sheer energy emanating from the participants, and also catching my breath as I'd just walked up a hill. That's what I love about France, you never know what you will find around the next corner.

In my absence, Jeff, who had remained on the boat, had heard a tap on the window and looked up to see a pair of legs in a rather short skirt. He opened the door to be greeted by a blonde lady, in heels who requested €70, not entirely sure what the €70 was for he asked her cautiously and was told it was for two nights mooring. As we were unable to reach either the water or the electric and couldn't get off the boat safely, he was more than a little peeved, we assumed that the part we were moored in, without any facilities was free as there wasn't any notices indicating otherwise. The Husband then asked whether she could provide him with some identification as frankly anyone could walk along and ask us for money, we had been moored somewhere previously where we were asked for contributions to the commune from a lady running a snack bar on the quay and ourselves and the other boaters had all given her a contribution, but she did empty the dustbins, this place didn't have any. She told him that she didn't have any identification and he told her that when I returned I would come to the office and pay her, assuming it was now open.

On my return, exhausted after my magical mystery tour of Avignon, I immediately went to the office and paid but I was still not happy that we had had to pay so much for such an appalling mooring, I was even more cross to discover a month later that friends had stopped there for a week in May for free. We were not staying another day, tomorrow we were going onto more uncharted waters, the Petite Rhone, tonight we would watch the disco boat go passed, the elegant diners across the water and pray for the wind to dissipate.

Chapter Five

In the Jungle

The wind continued throughout the night and until late morning, we finally pulled away from the harbour at 11.50, a very late start. We had a couple of small marinas highlighted as potential stops, one of them, the port of Vallabreques, looked the perfect spot for a Sunday afternoon but as we approached there was a barrier across the entrance, so we couldn't enter, and we were too big to moor on the finger pontoons, so yet again, we carried on our way. We soon found ourselves leaving the wide expanse of the Rhone to join the Petite Rhone, which provides the only link between the Rhone and the Canal du Rhone Sete. We would be joining the Canal du Rhone Sete, but not to follow the route to the Mediterranean but to the Canal du Midi and then further on to Aquitaine on the Canal Deux Mers to the Garonne.

 On our holiday by car, years previously, we had visited all the marinas on the way to the sea, but as you would expect, they were for sailing boats, not big old Tjalks like ours, although, we do have friends that had a similar boat with lee boards specially carved wooden boards that are lowered on a pivot, each side of the boat, to simulate a keel, which enables the unkeeled Tjalks to operate in sea conditions. They make me think of Viking ships, sailing to conquer, ours doesn't have them, and we are far too lily livered to go on the sea. It was visiting those ports, where fat bellied men basked in the afternoon sun in January, that drove the desire to head South, (for the sun, not the fat bellied men, I have one of those already) In January in Froncles, it took half an hour to put enough layers on, not to freeze for a walk in my snow boots. Quite understandably the ports are always all packed solid, with waiting lists of years, we had enquired for a place for our first boat, *Aqualife*, which was ten metres, and were told to write a letter enclosing a photograph with the application, our boat was clearly taking part in a beauty contest, and failed! It was something that I was then aware of, and with our current boat *Jantina*, we have a business card with her photo and our contact details. Evidently, she passes the test as we had a mooring the coming winter in Moissac, on the canal de Garonne, along with our friends Sally and Glenn and their two dogs *Haggis* and *Deliah*. *Bilbo* and *Haggis* are big buddies and I am expecting to spend the winter with a muddy dog in the wheelhouse as *Bilbo* always tends to get into trouble with *Haggis*. It is another five months until we are due to arrive in Moissac, and we have the Petite Rhone and three canals to travel on first, so I needed to stop looking at maps of where we are heading for, and concentrate on where we were currently.

We had studied the boating guidebooks and the Petite Rhone sounded quite dangerous, not for the current or the winds but for the shallow drafts, low bridge clearances. Warnings of possibly going aground were a regular feature. Photographs of wooden spits sticking up from the water in between the channels alarmed me. We both needed to have our wits about us, and a copy of the CEVNI, with the European Waterway signs to hand, something that we rarely looked at on our tame canals. It was lucky, that by some miracle, I had finally worked out how to use my binoculars. The Husband had spent years being frustrated with my inability to operate a simple set of binoculars to provide him with an adequate summary of the route ahead. Today, would be the day that it was necessary to have them glued to my face, to monitor and look out for the green and red marker posts indicating the edges of the channel. It was a waring day, despite the obvious dangers, it being a Sunday, we were met with the usual lunatics in speed boats, evidently unperturbed by the evil wooden spikes, waiting to sear a hole in the side of their plastic boats. For us, the wake, much harsher than that of a passenger boat, was strong enough to knock us off course. On spying one approaching, it would be time to run downstairs into the lounge and disconnect the television and lay it on the bed again, it was evidently going to be a rocky ride.

We were aware that mooring was limited on the Petite Rhone and had earmarked a place on the map, hoping desperately that it would be empty when we arrived. It was, and we tied up to a metal pontoon on the river. It is only when you stop that you get a true impression of the beauty of your surroundings, when you are cruising there are always other things to consider. Our impression upon entering the Petite Rhone was how it must be on the Amazon, the thick expanse of trees blanketing each side. The surroundings were untamed by human hands, and the cacophony of sound emanating from the trees was something I have only heard whilst watching nature documentaries, that we would now associate as the sound of the South.

The noise enveloped us, the silence contrasting with the loud chirping of insects. *Matilda* emerged from under a chair and tentatively crept across the deck, the noise making her curious but timid. We lifted her off onto the pontoon, but grass had grown through the metal squares and she was not keen to advance The Husband took out our branch croppers and trimmed back the overhanging branches on the metal staircase, then carried her to the top. I don't blame her, the squawking was eerie, I felt like a Tetradactyl was going to swoop down and steal her away, or me.

Bilbo and I had our first decent walk for days, enjoying the openness of the space after being trapped inside the city for the weekend. What we didn't realise was that we weren't totally alone, the fields backed onto farms, and we soon had a chorus of barking from the local dogs, I had other concerns. Having been in a town for a few days, and away from rural moorings for nearly two weeks, I had omitted to douse myself in insect repellent and soon became covered in bites as we walked around the field in the uncut grass. I had only just recovered from my session at Belleville sur Saone, searching for *Matilda*, a foresaw a sleepless night ahead, scratching my newly acquired bites. We made a quick return to the boat and put *Matilda* safely back inside and closed the mosquito screening, if there were as many bugs outside as we could hear, we didn't want to invite them to cruise to the Rhone Sete with us tomorrow. All night, I was singing the well-known Eighties song by *Tight Fit*, hope if there were any lions out there, they sleep tonight.

We left The Petite Rhone at the imposing St Gilles Lock, joining the canal du Rhone Sete. It was a very strange lock, as it was 12-metre-deep but there was little water in it. Variable weather fluctuations can result in perhaps as little as 50 cm of water and a maximum of 2.50 metres, it hardly seemed worth the effort, particular as it needed to be monitored by a member of staff. We were back under the jurisdiction of VNF, the usual company running the waterways, which meant that I no longer needed to go through three different announcements on the automated service when I wanted to speak to a lock keeper and they ignored my VHF radio. It also meant not logging onto the website to check the flow of the river. We would soon be back to relative safety, for a few days anyway.

St Giles lock evidentially served some purpose, closing the level of the Petite Rhone in the winter when the water level goes above 3.10 metres, after this puddle there wouldn't be any locks until we arrived at Sete, hurrah! I had been looking forward to joining the Canal du Rhone Sete. As we were coming closer to the sea, the water would be different, we needed to look out for barnacles and shingle, that was a first but most importantly, the Canal du Rhone Sete, would lead us to wildlife not seen in the rest of France. The Canal du Rhone Sete takes you through parts of The Camargue Regional Park. The promise of spying pink flamingos, wild horses and bulls, had been my incentive for this trip. The Camargue is predominantly low lying barren marshland, with a few sand dunes dotted around, in the summer it becomes a salty desert, with lakes retaining the saline water, creating a unique habitat for over three hundred and sixty species of birds. Growing up in the North East of England, I had been in the unusual position of living in an area where it was possible to see Flamingos and not after a few gin and tonics, or standing outside a seedy nightclub, a la Marc Almond from Soft Cell, but real life Pink Flamingos, in Flamingo land, in North Yorkshire. I anticipate that viewing them free from containment, from the deck of our boat, would be a slightly better experience than a family day out, complete with car sickness, on a damp day in Yorkshire!

Since we passed Lyon, The Husband and I had been repeatedly misquoting a line from 'The Fellowship of the Ring 'by JRR Tolkien, paraphrasing it to "It'll be the farthest I've ever been "but leaving the Petite Rhone to join the Rhone Sete, I truly felt that we were on our quest, but nothing quite as dramatic as throwing a ring into Mount Doom, but finding our winter mooring in the sun. It was our journey that was the adventure, as our quest will never end until we decide to hang up our life jackets for good, whenever that may be.

The entrance to the Canal du Rhone Sete, was a huge disappointment, we joined a canal with tatty, sometimes abandoned, boats, lining its side. First impressions, were, what a dump, we hoped it would improve as we continued. It was odd, for a none sailor, to be studying a map with the Mediterranean Sea indicated on the same page as running parallel and notices to beware of currents, I thought that was over with. The one relief was that no longer would I be looking out for giant cruise ships, but the screen on my AIS was full, with sailing boats, they would soon be joining a sea port and getting out their sails to join the Med at Sete, we would be crossing the Etang de Thau and waving goodbye to the sea to join the Canal du Midi. The first couple of ports were full of hire boats, the silly season hadn't quite started, so they weren't all let out, and there gathered a wall of abandoned white plastic, a blight on the landscape. By eleven we had arrived at the port of Gallician, we were unable to moor in the port as I had finger pontoons sticking out into the water, we have a large prop so cannot moor stern on (bum in to be less technical) so for the first time in an age, we chose to wild moor. It was quite tricky as the bank was uneven, and it was necessary for me to hang over the bow with my stick, poking to establish how much depth we had so we didn't go aground, the problem being is, this is nature, not a swimming pool, and the levels change, so after several failed attempts to get the stern in, as the water wasn't deep enough, we aborted and tried again further along the canal with better results. After swinging the bow in, I clamoured off the front, taking a rope with me, wrapped it round a boulder and then took one of our stakes and the sledge hammer from The Husband and then the stern rope. Our boat is extremely heavy and pulling it in is not fun, but the only way The Husband could get off to put a stake in, was if I held it and pulled it in. After some huffing and puffing, from both of us, we were securely moored up, *Matilda* would not be able to go out as we couldn't put a gangplank out as the bank was not level, but at least we were stopped in a tranquil environment and back to a canal.

Gallician was the perfect place for us to stay after the noise of Avignon with the traffic from the dual carriageway tearing passed all day and night, a continuous din of traffic lights, car engines and impatient drivers beeping in the continental way. The sounds of the city. Our position was next to the cycle track, so the only noise was the whirling of wheels and the chatter from cyclists to each other. The track, the Via Rhôna was recently built and followed the Rhone to Palavas les Flot, further along the Canal. Our friends, the cicadas were still chirping away but the trees had been cleared to make way for the cycle track, which was good for us as it meant that we were marginally less likely to be eaten alive today. Getting back into 'small village' mode, taking *Bilbo* for his necessaries, I went in search of the nearest boulangerie, forgetting that it was Monday, of course the boulangerie was at the other side of the village, but it gave me the chance to get my bearings. There was little I n the actual village, a village Épicerie, closed, a restaurant, closed until September, and a Wine cooperative, closed. What was open, was a tourist office/ shop, stacked with goodies. I quickly returned *Bilbo* to the boat and returned with my handbag. My intention was to buy some wine from every area to take home for my parents at the end of the summer. The Camargue is ideal for growing rice, and the salt extracted is considered a delicacy, both were on sale in the Tourist office, the wine was rather pricy, but I bought a couple of bottles, along with some wine and rice. The other local delicacies of Camargue Bull, were not my cup of tea, they are also bred for the bull fighting that takes place in the village, I am unsure as to where the bull ring was, but I certainly wouldn't endorse something so barbaric but when we are guests in a country, I have learnt to keep opinions to myself. I headed back to the boat, with a heavy bag and a lighter wallet, feeling the thrill of shopping, even for salt and rice. I would fall foul of the lure of the tourist shop on many occasions during the trip, my shopaholic tendencies may have been stifled due to my change in lifestyle, but, I 'm still me.

The advantages of having a large boat, is that you can wild moor and it is free, so the money you would have spent paying to be in on a clean pontoon, you can spend on locally, so the money goes to the local businesses, not the council. The disadvantage, is apart from the obvious throwing myself off at odd angles is that you don't get to talk to other people, sometimes this is ideal, some days you want to be on your own, tucked away somewhere. Due to our cat requirements, we will always moor away semi-rural, to allow our little tiger to roam free. In this instance, the port only had a couple of French boats permanently moored and unoccupied, so circumstances wouldn't be any different, but ours friends stayed in Gallician for two weeks and had a wonderful time, but they were in a sail boat, which is cheap to moor and the harbour was full, the experience was poles apart. However, as we couldn't moor in the port we wouldn't have been able to stop if we hadn't got the equipment and the wherewithal to moor up on the side. I would have missed my shopping experience and it would be one of those places, that looked nice, marked on the map that I looked at regret that we hadn't been able to stop, again.

By lunchtime, we were bored, the adrenalin charging through us to get to the next leg of the journey. After lunch, we were surprised to find a large hotel barge passed us, we didn't think they would be able to get through, our stakes were not in the ground as much as we thought, so more fiddling around to re secure them. Not long after, a restaurant/disco boat, came passed, and then came back. We would soon realize that this was not unusual sight in this region. We had seen restaurant boats many times before but until that time I haven't ever seen a boat, packed with pensioners, dancing, in the middle of the afternoon, in the sun. They looked like they were having great fun, when the boat returned they were still dancing, good on them, I was ready for an afternoon nap.

With not much to do apart from walking up and down the canal, limited as most of it was cycle track, and we only had one bike, we made an early start the next morning, to avoid the heat of the afternoon sun. Our next stop would be Palavas le Flot. We had been travelling a short distance, I was in the galley, cleaning up after breakfast, when The Husband called me to come upstairs, staring through my window, close enough to see their glistening nostrils, were the Camargue wild horses I had been waiting to see. Obviously, over the years of cruising, we have seen a selection of animals from the deck, but the Camargue wild horses are like the Dartmoor ponies, a precious entity.

By lunchtime we found ourselves in Palavas les Flots, a seaside town, the sky shone brightly a cerulean blue and gulls wheeled beneath it. Entering from the direction of the canal, you could be forgiven in thinking that the seaside was a distant spot on the horizon as it is located on a strip of land between the Mediterranean Sea and the wild, natural, briny ponds. Upon arriving I initially failed to see the beauty of the locality. A long concrete quay with bollards provided adequate mooring without the need for acrobatics but securing the lines proved tricky as the corpse of a seagull managed to lodge itself in-between the boat and the wharf. Combined with the overflowing rubbish bins along the walk way, first impressions were disappointing. After using the engine to dislodge our feathered visitor we tied up. The squeamish townie I had once been was long gone, after digging ditches for dead fish, a decapitated seagull was unpleasant, but my old reaction of disgust, was overtaken by anger that someone had caused this, whether a boat had hit the poor bird, or it had died because of the rubbish I don't know, but I was very cross. In front of us was a hotel barge carrying about eighteen passengers, I expect the reason for the overflowing bins, as it left not long afterwards.

Putting aside our initial reaction that Palavas was a dump, we took *Bilbo* for a stroll along the promenade and spied the sandy beaches and a lighthouse across the vista. The resort was within walking distance, if that's your thing.

For us, the second treat of the day, was glimpsing the flock of pink flamingoes in the marsh.it wasn't until I took a stroll to the supermarket that I discovered more flamingoes across the horizon and a fruit stall, in a layby, something that would become a familiar sight. Seeing the flamingoes in their natural habitat was remarkable, had we been the correct size to moor in the harbour, we may well have missed them, but in our dirty mooring, rubbish spilling across the footpath, we were able watch them at our leisure, as they flew off and returned to their resting place.

The stretch along the canal was scattered with summer houses in pastel colours, platforms overhanging the water, little boats tied up at the end of the spits. We were leaving the Med, but this was our South of France. In one day we had seen two wondrous sights, and we would drift off to sleep with the lights from the revolving tower, known as The Lighthouse of the Mediterranean, flashing through the windows, the faint sound of music and the odour of seaweed wafting towards us, and pink flamingoes by our windows. We had been travelling for two weeks and entered another world, a separate part of France.

Waking to the sun shining vibrantly, we set off to the town of Frontignan, another town of contrasts. The beach of Frontignan plage, was a bus ride away, but we are not great lovers of beaches, having both grown up by the sea. The mooring was interesting in that if approached from the direction of Palavas les Flot, with falling down fisherman's cottages, smelly sand dunes and a general feeling of neglect, you are stuck moored on a concrete quay and prevented from furthering your journey by a bridge that only opens twice a day. We were able to tie up, but *Matilda* was unable to explore as the quay was situated next to a road with traffic tearing passed, so a disgruntled cat for the day. However, the extreme heat was probably enough to prevent her from venturing far, we had the same feeling. By lunch time the hire boaters were chomping at the bit, desperate to get through and continue their journey. We opted to remain moored for the day and observe what happened, on the other side of the bridge was a small port, full and not suited to our size so when we passed through we needed to continue to the next stop, not achievable at 4 pm, the next bridge opening. After lunch I decided to head into town. I was intrigued at the building on the other side of the water and I needed to get some shopping, the previous days trip I had succeeded in buying little as there was a cycle track, but not a footpath and the dangerous journey on foot had dissuaded me from purchasing too much as I needed to focus on getting back safely, not on heavy bags.

The interesting building was a wine house, another cooperative and a distillery. Muscat de Frontignan, a dessert wine is produced there. The name had been familiar to be, but I assumed it was because I had been studying the maps and recognized it.it was other studying that I spent much more effort on, the wine sections. I remembered the distinguishable bottle, and the sweet tasting wine. I chose not to investigate, the Husband most certainly wouldn't accompany, he was on red alert, as I had come across a gyspy camp opposite to where we were moored, had I not taken *Bilbo* for a walk, I would have been oblivious, but on my return, we had spent some time, moving everything stealable inside. Sometimes it's better not to know these things, but having had items stolen from the boat on numerous occasions, we always take precautions, the effort of putting everything away, is less than the annoyance of having something stolen, however insignificant.

So not wine tasting, or museum browsing, supermarket searching. I found one on my walk into town, but it was closed, until next week. Had I not lived in France, I would have found this ridiculous but now, a Gaelic shrug. We will not starve, off for some sightseeing. Sadly, the old town Centre, was dilapidated, a real disappointment. A museum and chapel, closed, but great architecture. I suppose we should be heading to the beaches not looking at old buildings, that's where the people that work there probably are, on their sail boats, keeping cool.

I returned with only a few cans of soft drinks and some sickly-looking cakes, they looked appetising in the window, but they seemed to have collapsed in the heat. We ate them anyway but what I really wanted was an ice cream, but it would have been terribly mean to eat one in town and it would be melted by the time I got back wouldn't it? With a cold drink, we waited to see the chaos that was about to occur. Hire boaters trying to overtake each other and block off the entrance to the bridge, naively oblivious that on the other side was almost a mirror of events, so that as the bridge went up, everyone tried to get through the same piece of water. Two boys played on some pedaloes for hire, chained up, they jumped across each one then dived into the water, hoisting themselves back on to the boats, causing them to bash the boats into each other. No one seem to care, apart from *Bilbo*, who took offence at the little hooligans, barking, he obviously has a better set of morals than the locals. Instead of lying in the shade, I had to put him inside, as it was more likely someone would complain to us about him.

The bridge went up and the boats all set off, next to us swapped one set of white plastic boats for another, some keen to keep going for the rest of the day and others to stop and explore the town. While the bridge was up, the car drivers sat impatiently, car stereos blazing, some beeping their horns, rather pointlessly. Combined with the racket the trains were making, rattling overhead, it was not a peaceful mooring, no wonder the town was abandoned, I couldn't wait to abandon it. After returning for a leisurely walk amongst the sand and seaweed, when temperatures had dropped, we locked the doors and stayed inside. The signs warning car owners to be vigilant of thieves, plastered on all the lampposts not reassuring us that we were moored in a good area for the night. Rich pickings with hire boaters on holiday leaving bikes unchained on the deck or worse, outside leaning against a lamppost. I am not sure I am going to like the South.

Our boat had an alarm, and around eleven thirty that evening a group of teenagers were sitting on the wall outside our boat. We had set the alarm hours before, and when one decided to have a peak into our boat they got the shock of their lives, they all ran rapidly away. We were aware they were outside by their loud chattering and were hoping they would sit somewhere else, so we could go to bed, perhaps we need to accidently set the alarm off the next time someone Is being a nuisance.

So, the next morning found us waiting for the morning opening of the Frontignan Bridge at 8.30 am, from watching the previous evenings opening it was obvious the many hireboats could be quite aggressive in their attempts to be first to the limited moorings on each side. We however were aiming for a crossing of the infamous Etang De Thau, a shallow 15 km. long lake with huge oyster beds on its northern side. The lake is subject to frequent high winds which make it dangerous to cross, so we were lucky the forecast was for a reasonably calm day. I secretly wished at this time we were travelling in our old cruiser, not because *Jantina* was not capable of making the journey, we had survived the mighty Rhone, but because the Etang De Thau had places inaccessible to us in our beast. We were probably able to visit from a size point of view, but I suspect, our boat was just not posh enough.

Years ago, Rick Stein the Cornish chef, produced a television series called 'The French Odyssey', the second part of his journey was on the Canal du Midi to Toulouse on a series of hotel barges with his crew. As I am not a big foodie, and as The Husband and I don't eat fish, which he is famous for, it is not something I would have made an effort to watch. I hadn't seen this at the time of transmission, I suspect I was struggling with local cuisine myself, but a good friend of my mother's mentioned it to me on one of her visits to our home, as she and her husband are big Rick Stein fans, visiting his restaurant in Padstow annually. I bought the DVD and suspect, due to his global appeal, one of the reasons there are so many people on boats in France from other countries. Travelling in your own boat is not the same as being crewed and waited on but you have your own itinerary. I chose to watch the DVD over the winter, creating a romantic image of boating and making us desperate to get out on the water. His filming of the Etang de Thau, with the oyster beds, had given us a sneak preview of the crossing, obviously with a skilled skipper. We had also had a cheeky look when we holidayed in Arles, never imagining we would ever make the crossing ourselves, we were still on our first canal boat, and hadn't the time to invest in such a long trip from the North, it was simply, as Kenneth Grahame's Ratty so eloquently put it for' messing about in'.

The Etang du Thau is thought to be the second saltwater largest lake in France. We had lived near to the largest artificial/fresh water lake in Europe,

Lac du der de Chantecoq but had only been on the water in hire boats several times, in fact, The Husband hadn't ever been on it, as both encounters, The Daughter and I had been with friends during the holidays, whilst he was working at our lakes. Our daughter had even been taught to sail, by her school there, something that would come in very handy, should we ever buy a sail boat. It was another nearby lake, Lac Amance, that had led us to purchasing our first speed boat, finding that we tired quickly of the largest motorboat lake in Europe we went on to the more genteel method of boating, along the canals. Today would have been a good day to have had our first boat for tearing about in.

On the eastern side of the Etang du Thau, a narrow strip of headland with golden sand separates the Etang du Thau from the Mediterranean. Each of the small towns, nestling on the edges of the Etang du Thau, hold hidden delights. There's Bouzigues, where famous oysters are produced has a museum, and the obligatory restaurants for sampling the local delicacies. Balaruc les Bains, the second largest spa in Europe and Sete, encircling the Mont St Clair, which is famous for its summer boat jousting. Red and blue boats take part in a yearly festival, and my favourite Marseillan. We had driven to Marseillan on the way back from one of our holidays in Spain, specifically to find if it was possible for a mooring. With virtually year-round sun and a hop across to Spain, it seemed ideally situated for us to make our winter home. However, we received a less that welcome reception from one of the English residents on their boat. I am unsure whether it was our scruffy dog that made the man visibly turn his nose up at us, our that fact that we were driving a Seat Altea, not a Mercedes, (albeit only a couple of years old at the time, so hardly an old heap). It couldn't have been our barge, as there was a similar model to ours moored, but with the wing shaped lee boards for sailing attached, so obviously he didn't like the look of us. Perhaps it was our glowing tans in February, we had just spent six weeks in the sun. He was working on his boat, and I enquired if he could point me in the direction of the Capitain office. He rudely responded that the office was closed, but we wouldn't get a mooring, and that the Captain only spoke French. My husband, replied that I spoke French, so that wouldn't be a problem and ignored his stand-offish behavior and asked him about the port itself. Usually, people are more than happy to tell you how wonderful their mooring is, then gleefully remark that there isn't any space. We thanked him for his time, and strolled around the port with *Bilbo*, taking note of the Captains details from the door. The port was fairly pricey, as to be expected in the Med, but the man who spoke to us had a boat that was nothing to write home about, so they obviously weren't that fussy, our previous boats had all been far nicer. But perhaps he was what my friend Karen used to describe as 'A Pissy old man, on a pissy old boat', there's a lot of them about. Marseillan itself was an attractive port and a protected heritage site, I would anticipate the town mainly buzzed during the summer, as it appeared to mostly be holiday homes, and boats, so perhaps it would have been a mistake to moor there for the winter, but at least it would have been warm! The Noilly Prat company are based there, and a visitor centre is set up on the quay. It all looked very charming, but with reviews in both the English newspapers The Telegraph and The Guardian, perhaps that's why the people moored their thought they were in what was described as St Tropez before Bardot, I think that was a little over exaggeration, or am I being bitter because we couldn't get it. With our speed boat, we could have stopped had a glorious lunch, with our last cruiser, we could have sat on our deck overlooking the harbour, pretending we were really in St Tropez, instead we must continue onto the Canal du Midi, to mix with the flotilla of plastic hire boats, as sensible boaters would not choose to cruise on the Midi in July.

We made our way through the bridge and proceeded along the 6-km. stretch of canal to the lake. The route across the lake is marked by Red and Green buoys, which even through binoculars proved quite difficult to follow, they averaged more than 2km to 3km distant. Luckily there was a large privately-owned sea going cruiser about a kilometre ahead who obviously knew the way and fortuitously was brilliant white. The pine covered hill at Sete was now in the distance. We increased speed to our maximum about 13kph and just managed to keep her in sight before spying the last buoys situated at the lighthouse which marks the entrance to the World-Famous Canal Du Midi.

The Canal du Midi has been a UNESECO World Heritage Site since 1996, plane and oak trees were planted along the towpaths to provide shade for the horses towing the barges. We had walked along the Canal du Midi, many times but this would be our first experience by boat. The camera was at the ready for our first glimpse, having mentally ticked off another achievement, The Etang de Thau, I was bubbling with anticipation, this was what we set off for three plus months ago. Every day, I marked off our progress on our map of the European Waterways. There are lots of beautiful parts of France, we have been fortunate that we have visited many, although, it would take many years to visit them all. An Anglo-French Newspaper, which I have been reading since we first moved to France, published a list in the June edition, of the top must visit places in France. The Canal du Midi was always on that list, and I suspect always will be, although other places are changed every year.

The entrance was not what we expected, there was a sailing club and then numerous smallish boats, many in poor states of repair a few which had been left to rot and at least two that had actually sunk. The first few kilometres progressed through a salt marsh until we reached the first Midi lock. The locks on the Midi are all operated by lock keepers and because of their unique oval shape can accommodate up to four 12-meter boats at one time, priority is given to Hotel Barges but although at over 20 metres we are classed as a large vessel strictly we do not have similar benefits. Fortunately, we were the only boat in the first two locks. It was as we approached I was quickly removing the washing that I had hung on the rails to dry whilst we crossed the Etang, I needed to be able to access all sides of the boat without getting a pair of pants in my face as I ran across the deck. Passing through the second lock took us onto a short section of the Herault River then back onto the canal and the Round lock of Agde taking us to the town of Agde, another town with a fabulous beach not far away. As one of the larger and more well-known towns we were hoping to moor but first we had to tackle a unique lock. As we often do if possible, when we approach something unusual, we tie up and study the best way to approach it. With the lock at Agde there was great mooring space before the lock, so we tied up, got *Bilbo* off the boat, and walked up to see how it was done. The lock was operated by a lock keeper, and we arrived at lunchtime, giving ourselves time to look without interfering with anyone's boating. After a brief discussion, we were walking back to the boat and a conversation arose with an English couple who lived in the town and were fascinated by our boat. Lunch break was nearly over, so we excused ourselves and I jokingly said please don't watch us, as having someone staring at you is very off putting, especially if they try and talk to you whilst you are in the lock.

What makes the lock unusual, is firstly, as its name suggests, it is round, which allows the boat to turn around. Secondly, it has three sets of gates, at three different water levels. You must tell the lock keeper where you want to go so she can decide where to put you, and when. We were continuing onto Beziers on the Canal du Midi, but it is also possible to go onto the Herault River. When the lock keeper arrived, I walked back to the lock and asked her if we could enter and explained how long we were. For the shorter hire boats, it is possible to squeeze a lot of them in and they can fit in on different parts of the lock. We had worked out where we wanted to go and how to hold the boat securely. We entered the lock and I put a rope on the stern and the bow. Other boats came in, them when she decided to activate the lock, she walked past and took the rope off the bollard it was on and put it on another one the result being as the lock filled, our boat scissored across the lock, scaring the pants out of the plastic boaters and causing alarm for both of us. She had moved the rope from a bollard on a high wall to a lower wall, which was at the centre of our boat, leaving the stern untethered. There were many onlookers, and when new exited the lock, I commented to The Husband, that we would probably appear on YouTube, we were both extremely cross at the lock keeper as she had caused us to damage our boat.

We were now in Agde, but the moorings suitable for our type of boat were taken up for commercial boats, restaurant boats, hotel barges, we couldn't moor in the port, so we carried along a little way and moored along a bank. That evening, we would see a disorderly queue of glammed up people waiting on the quay to dinner and dance on one of the restaurant boats, a strange selection, with a mother and grown up daughter and some single men, perhaps it was a dating boat. It was my second attempt at wild mooring and I had worked out one thing, wear jeans and a long sleeved top and gloves. The brambles were a nightmare, no longer my delicate deck shoes for jumping around the boat, but trainers with thick soles to protect myself from thorns. After initially securing a rope around a tree whilst I pulled the stern in, we got tied up on stakes, and decided to take a couple of days off in Agde, The Husband wanted to find a chandlery, I think we needed some paint.

Matilda was delighted, as we were moored in the wilderness, gang plank out and off she went. *Bilbo* was equally as happy, walking had been limited the day before, now we were in the woods, we could walk in the shade. On our first walk, we encountered, what I call a Krusties Camp. Krusties, are, what is politely termed as travellers. Not gypsies, who are a totally different ball game. Travelers live alternative lifestyles, think Johnny Depp in *Chocolat*, some people consider that we live an alternative lifestyle living on our boat, we have definitely dropped out of society to live an unconventional existence, luckily, we don't have to fund it by selling crafts, which is a good thing as I am not very crafty, although in my head I think I am and would love to be. It's a little like the ideal of the impoverished artist, we like the idea, but most people don't desire to live like a student all their life. To come across a community of people living in the woods, my reaction couldn't have been more different to the previous day, when I came across a gyspy camp. We couldn't get away fast enough!

Our new neighbours seemed to be living in a selection of tee pees, bunting hanging from the trees and a few scruffy dogs wandering around. There wasn't rubbish anywhere, the place was spotless. One of the residents set up every morning along the track with drawings from a van, a girl sold things made from wood. I think the van went back into the camp at night as they would be packing up as I walked *Bilbo*, and I stopped and chatted. It's strange how we react in certain ways, as one of the gypsies from the camp near our lake used to cycle down to the port and try and sell baskets to the boaters, I saw it as a ruse to make an assessment what was available to steal, I would be as likely to chat to him as set him on fire, pre- conceptions.

So, content in our woodland idyll, we set off in search of a chandlery, The Husband was also not perturbed by the camp, but that has taken some years to instill a lack of suspicion, it's an age thing as much as anything, as I grew up when friends were protesting at hunts, and climbing trees, attending illegal raves in farmers' fields, you couldn't get much further from that in Essex. As expected the chandlery had closed down, another derelict building, so we set off look for one in the town and see the sea.

Across a bridge a magnificent cathedral overlooked the river Herault. It was only 2 kilometres from the Mediterranean Sea, and the river was lined with small boats heading off for Cap d' Agde. I was captivated by its charm, so much so that I suggested we bought a sail boat and kept it there for the summer. I do tend to get carried away with things. Of course, the difference between us and normal people is we actually consider it as opposed to throw away comments, not meant seriously. The narrow winding streets held nothing particular of interest, apart from tiny art galleries. On not such a cheerful note, on researching places to visit whilst we were there, I found that in the second world war perhaps two thousand Jews were deported from Germany and Austria to a labour camp near the town. We tend to not associate the South of France with such atrocities but sadly it is everywhere, we just don't know it.

Mission unsuccessful, we availed ourselves of some funds at the fruit and vegetable stall, permanently erected on the main road, just above The Round Lock, conveniently selling soft drinks and wine too, you could almost be mistaken for thinking you were in a tourist resort! We headed back to the boat, to live in the woods for a day, and with the exception of a disco boat, passing us in the dark, without any external lights, we hardly heard a sound, only the birds chirping. What more could you ask for.

Chapter Six

"Crash, Bang Wallop, What a Picture"

We had made it to the promised land, the Canal du Midi, today would be our first day on the boating bucket list. As our first day was a Saturday, we made the sensible decision to find the first mooring and stop. Saturday, usually being changeover day for the hire boat companies, we did not wish to find ourselves sharing a lock with a family who had just collected their boat. We were always working weekends when we had our previous boats, so managed to escape that pleasure mostly , although we have been witness to a few mishaps, one turning round completely in the middle of the lock and exiting the way they came in, an idiotic father letting his small son operate the controls and pressing the red button instead of the green, causing the lock to go into 'lockdown' and all the boats in the lock having to wait for an eclusier to come and reprogram the lock, and on one occasion, a German man, hitting us, an hour after collecting the boat for holiday (a mid weeker,we were caught out !)

The first proper Midi lock was at a little place called Portiragnes, back to normal size at 2.33 meres deep, but unlike the locks we were used to slightly oval, and operated by a lock keeper. We hadn't had the luxury of mooring and looking at the lock so work out beforehand and we floundered as to where to sit in the lock, our boat too long to sit in the middle like the hire boats, and with the walls higher on the straight part. We swapped the ropes for longer ones, but the position the lock keeper wanted us we were not happy with as it left us with the stern swinging in and out as we were not flat against it. When it's not your own boat, unless you do major damage then there is little concern for the welfare of the boat, we had frequently witnessed one of the major companies attending call outs on the Saone where various engine parts had burnt out through over/misuse. If their boats had scratches and dents they didn't care. However, we did, we had been told by a friend that as we were over twenty metres we could refuse to go into a lock if we weren't happy, it wasn't something we intended doing but the next morning we employed a different tactic, letting other boats go ahead. It of course didn't work as there were too many boats we wouldn't have ever got anywhere, but we tried.

We left the lock, not satisfied with our performance, or the attitude of the lock keeper, he blatantly ignored our request to moor so we sat against the curve of the lock, so he could shove another boat behind us, thus damaging our boat, again. Twice in two days, this didn't bode well. We moored up on pins along the canal, in what we hoped was a peaceful spot. Running along the top of the bank was a cycle track, it being Saturday morning people were running and cycling along the designated area. We had our pins in the long grass, foot high silver stakes, someone decided to detour the track and run down the bank and promptly fell over our bright yellow ropes. It was going to be one of those days.

There was little to see in Portiragnes, a blink and you miss it village, situated along the Canal du Midi, with another fruit and veg stall, we certainly weren't going to get scurvy on this trip. The main feature of the village, was that you could drive to the beach. Once the runners and cyclists had done their weekend stint, the afternoon quietened, and we barely saw a person until early the following morning. Waking to another blue sky, I was almost missing waking to a thick wall of cloud, a reprise from the heat would have been pleasant. As I took *Bilbo* for his morning walk, I came upon a girl of about nineteen, with long blonde tousled hair, wearing very little clothing, she had a blanket over and was laying on the bank. As we drew nearer, she got up, lit a cigarette, wrapped her blanket around her and staggered off, we continued along the canal path and she disappeared, you do see some strange sights, particularly early in the morning, as there was only canal path I couldn't fathom where she had gone but hoped it was somewhere safe. A least a car couldn't have passed and taken her off, but I was unsettled all day that this girl had eerily vanished into thin air.

There weren't any locks on the next stretch to the town of Villeneuve sur Beziers. We had walked along this stretch of the canal many times on visits by car, and were hoping to get a mooring if we arrived early enough, the balancing act of what time others leave, creating a gap to moor, and not arriving too close to lunch as it will be full. Villeneuve is a cute little town with a small supermarket and a few shops. I knew it would be pricey, but supplies were running low, the heat making us guzzle cold drinks to keep hydrated, and of course, we were out of wine. The eternal boater conundrum, do you carry a bottle of wine and a carton of milk and some orange juice, or give up on the orange juice, so you can buy food. Sadly, for me it is Diet Coke that I tipple but if I came back with diet coke and not wine then I would not be welcomed warmly. Luckily, we got moored within walking distance, and I made several trips to the shop as we had no idea when we would next stop near a shop. The square, which we had not visited previously, was your usual small French square. Surrounded by trees and a few benches dotted about, on Sundays, (which it was) it held the added attraction of the market, a few stalls but nevertheless a bonus, and as the mooring was free, an opportunity to put a little bit back. I later discovered that this wasn't the actual market, but an extra seasonal one, so we had been lucky to come upon it. I much prefer buying eggs with a feather or two in the box and cheese and pate that aren't covered in plastic film. As the heat was intense, The Husband decided we should leave after lunch, unlike Portiragnes, we hadn't any tree cover, since our last visit to the Midi, the trees were starting to be culled and the bank was bare. A blight, blamed on the Americans, importing ammunition in wooden trunks in the war, allegedly brought a disease to France. But then of course, they would be speaking German now and I don't suppose we would be boating in France, so I think that the French got a better deal, if there is any truth to the story at all!

Villeneuve les Beziers was originally a roman settlement, it's the great thing about France, even the little villages are steeped in history. For us there were more modern sights to see. On one bank was a campsite and boats moored all along, one boat covered in camouflage netting, further along, in front of a pretty restaurant with an already bustling terrace, were a selection of small day hire electric boats. I would soon learn that on the Midi, there are boats everywhere, of all shape and sizes. Moored in front of us was a prettily painted wooden boat, on closer inspection, I found it was a Tourism boat for the Canal du Midi, it reminded me of when our daughter was a small child and we use to take her to the Ragdoll shop in Stratford upon Avon, where a replica narrowboat stood for children to climb about and pretend they were Rosie and Jim, I hadn't ever anticipated that one day we would have our own, slighter larger, old boat.

 The Tourist boat, was travelling up and down the canal du Midi, I hadn't taken much notice of it when it was in Agde, but I had a quick look in Villeneuve les Beziers, it was a fascinating collection of black and white photos of the canal, time was tight as we needed to be ready for the lock to open but I intended on returning again, the next time I came across it. The concept was a great idea, a moveable tourist office, stashed full of info for all the canal users, not just the boaters.

We pulled across to the other side of the canal to a wall in front of the entrance to the lock, to wait for it to open and a chap came over and asked us if we wanted to buy any books as one of the boats along the quay was a 'Book Boat', we declined, I would have been in trouble if the lock opened and I was off buying books. Behind us, three hire boats were revving there engines as if they were at the front of the grid at Monaco, I could see we what fun lay head. As the lock, opened we proceeded to enter and I began to attach the ropes back onto our bollards. Our usual procedure of powering onto the front rope was not possible as we would create too much wash behind for other boats so we both were a little hesitant, The Husband called down that I should put a longer rope on the high bollard at the front of the bow, so as I moved the rope we heard a crash. A hire boat had advanced forward, not taking into account our position and had shunted our rudder. They hit us so hard that they broke the flag pole clean off the rudder. The Husband, ran out of the wheelhouse, onto the deck to see what the noise/damage was. Realising that they had hit us, the boat then reversed out of the lock, but not before The Husband shouted that I would come and find them for their insurance details, and something not very polite. We exited the lock, and after several failed attempts, I managed to find somewhere relatively safe to jump off and get some stakes in to secure the boat.

As you would expect in July, in the South of France, it was blisteringly hot, after my attempts to jump off, I was hot and bothered, the last thing I wanted to do was have an argument with someone. I had been taking photos earlier in the day, so the camera was close to hand and I had taken several photos of the damage, I had also scribbled down the make of the hire boat and model, as I was evidently going to play hunt the hire boat as it had decided to hide from view, amongst all the others as it had not advanced through the lock with the next set of boats but stayed on the other side.

I scrambled off the boat and walked back to the lock, a woman with a purpose. I had my folder with our insurance documents and as I approached the bridge over the lock, I scanned the water for the hire boat. Once I identified it, I marched towards it steam coming out of my ears. One of the reasons we had sold our business was to reduce stress, on the infrequent times we had a difficult client's confrontation made The Husband ill. I could see his point, my heart was pounding but we had no idea how much damage had been done to the rudder, until we were moored somewhere suitable, so it was essential to get the insurance details.

As I approached the boat, there were several people aboard. I explained who I was, in a calm fashion and requested their insurance details, writing down the serial number on the side of the boat. Instead of apologising, a woman shouted

"Your husband was very rude"

At which I replied,

"You hit our boat, full on, it's hardly surprising, can I have your details please"

The woman ignored my request and proceeded to tell me that she had hired a boat on the Canal du Midi for the previous three years, she knew what she was doing.

I replied, *"we had done over one hundred locks already this year, had five boats in France and had brought our boat from Holland, that having two weeks a year on a hire boat was hardly the same, and please could she give me her details"*

She refused again, then her husband stepped in, and said *"For goodness sake, give the woman the insurance details, you hit their boat"*

Eventually, she folded and gave me their details, still shouting that she had years of experience.

We didn't file a claim, that evening The Husband sawed our flagpole in half and repaired it. We had had our first altercation on the Canal du Midi, on our second day. It didn't bode well. I can't say we were totally blameless but the felt that the lock keeper should have waited until our ropes were secure before allowing a boat in behind us, as we soon found, the lock keepers on the Canal du Midi, didn't give a hoot about private boats, they wanted us all out as soon as we were able, to chunt us through on the conveyor belt of hire boats that is the Canal du Midi. We couldn't totally avoid being in locks with hire boats, but we would try our best to wherever possible, and hope for the best.

Villeneuve Les Beziers

Two more locks before we were would find a mooring for the night in the city of Beziers, we needed to stop in Beziers as we had left our car in Macon three weeks ago and The Husband was intending on catching the train back the following morning, we were keeping our fingers crossed that it would still be there, I had left in the car park at Macon port, not an unusual thing for boaters to do, we leave our cars all over, but at least ours was French registered so not quite as noticeable as a Uk registered one.

I wasn't overly keen on stopping in Beziers, the port did not have a good reputation, neither did the town. Beziers was our regular stop off point on our holidays in Spain. Just outside Beziers, down a private road is a Dog B and B, ran by two English guys, it became our go to place for *Bilbo*, his home from home. Whilst we got a week away in the warmth, he got the opportunity to stay in a house with four or five other dogs and play all day, his holiday. From our conversations with the owners, we had inside information on Beziers, the usual tales of theft and vandalism. As I have mentioned before, if you don't know, you can live in happy oblivion, but we had heard stories of cars in restaurant car parks with tyres removed whilst the owners ate inside and had witnessed the usual groups of men hanging around in bars, intimidating the other clients so they drank up and left. I wasn't cherishing spending a day in port on my own.

Once we moored up in Beziers port, our priority was to locate the train station and purchase a ticket for The Husband for the following morning, we didn't want to stay in Beziers longer than necessary, and it would take him most of the day to get to Macon by train and then drive back, providing the car was still there, and started. The train station, as you would expect for a main hub in the South, was bustling, even on a Sunday afternoon, bus stops lined the entrance, crossing was rather precarious as the footpath was narrow, certainly not wide enough for the volume of people pushing through, the French have appalling manners, they can't queue, will never give way, and I have seen a man push a woman with buggy down a flight of narrow stone steps, rather than give way and wait for her to get to the top and we found ourselves walking on the road, which was the exit for the buses. I hastened to add, I have seen the same thing on a bus in Sheffield, with a friend with a buggy, some people are just rude, but having had a door slammed in my face, rather than hold it open and pass it, after ten years, I am not generalising, that's why I hate cities, unless I am on my own, as it's easier to slip through when there is only one of you. It's magnified by the quantity of people and the haste that everyone is in.

The area around the train station was not a complement to Beziers, it reflected my opinion of the place. Having driven round Beziers countless times, I marveled at the beauty of the Cathedral Saint Nazaire, overlooking the Orb river, visible from the motorway in the distance, its imposing presence inviting visitors to view the glories within. Regretfully, driving through the ring road of Beziers, the usual array of kebab shops, peeling posters and decrepit buildings did little to entice me to explore. The port was overlooked by a series of modern office blocks and apartments, separated by hedging and trees, sadly not providing any shade to the port but creating a sheltered walkway, doubtless the idea when the constructions opposite were planned. Crossing the road, it was a short walk to the station, under a bridge and the station to your left, a large shopping mall to your right, complete with hypermarket, all very convenient. The buildings opposite the train station were a series of tatty cafes and bars, the usual undesirable gangs of males hanging about outside. I certainly wouldn't be taking that route into town. Shining through the dross was the entrance to the *Plateau des Poetes*, with vintage style funfair, pony rides and puppet shows. Not something that I had need of but for all the hire boaters, overflowing with offspring, a great way of letting off steam, if you didn't get run over walking there. For adults, a romantic walk in the shade, in wonderful gardens. A flyer on the entrance gates for weekly Jazz concerts on Sunday evenings in July and August appealed, but not this Sunday, we were far too hot and bothered. We returned to the boat, and watched the fun unfold before our eyes.

It is quite normal to arrive at a port and find an area reserved for 'Bateau de plaisance', it could be for restaurant boats, day trip boats or hotel barges. Bezier being one of the hot tourist spots on The Canal du Midi, the Birthplace of Pierre Paul Riquet, who designed The Canal Du Midi, understandably, half the quay was reserved. As most of the port was full of hireboats on one side, and permanently moored boats on the opposite bank, we managed to squeeze in between two spaces reserved for bateau de plaisance, in this instance the signs specified the size of the boats, so we were able to measure exactly that we had left enough space on both side and were within the boundaries. For a Sunday afternoon in July, the Capitain was surprisingly absent, the office closed and no supervision. We didn't need water or electricity so were more than happy to tuck ourselves out of the way. As we left to walk to the train station, a large hire boat pulled in and tied up in the middle of the reserved area, I had suggested that I explain to them that could not moor there, but The Husband told me to not interfere, I thought I was being helpful as it would only end in tears.

It was evident that the occupants of the hire boat had gone out, perhaps to the funfair, as the lock opened a' Bateau de plaisance' exited with passengers. The other space had already been occupied by a restaurant boat, the staff preparing for the evening sitting. I am sure that it is not the first time that this has happened, but the Captain of the boat was understandably very cross, his crew were shouting, hire boats keen to get to the next lock, having exited the previous one, with nowhere to stop, tried to get around the boat, which was now sitting in the centre of the canal, engines revving, smoke billowing out.

The family appeared and nonchantly got back on the boat to meet a mouthful of abuse from the crew members, they hastily untied and advanced to queue up for the lock and the Bateau de plaisance pulled in so quickly, they set it careering across the canal, I think that in this instance, a little interfering may have been wise, although they may have ignored me anyway. Our first full day cruising on the Midi, I now understood why everyone complained about the hire boats, without any etiquette for the water, as they have no responsibility for their actions, they could do what they want, and annoy the pants out of us private boaters and we would soon find that the Bateau de Plaisance, ruled the waterways.

Entertainment over, after dinner the local gypsies arrived to wander up and down the quay, I too was wandering up and down with *Bilbo* under the shade of the trees, set further back from the quay, undoubtedly to buffer some of the road noise. The pavement was incredibly hot, it was great in the shade, but the company wasn't so welcomed. For them it was easy pickings along the quay, bikes left unattended by boats, phones and computers left on the deck when people went inside. It's hardly surprising the magpies were circling. We followed our usual produce of putting away everything stealable inside the wheelhouse, lifebuoys, sledgehammers, locked the doors and set the alarm.

Early the following morning, The Husband set off for his journey and I investigated the other side of the canal with *Bilbo* before the searing sun sent us inside for shelter. I had intended on a morning of culture, after I had caught up with some washing, but it was so hot on the deck it was unbearable. I hung my washing out along the rails and felt nauseous, walking around a stuffy gallery wasn't tempting. I would soon discover that if we weren't cruising we would spend much of the day, hidden inside, keeping cool. We were used to the heat in France but being in a house is not the same as a boat. At our home, we had shutters and kept the house deliciously cool. The last summer we had cruised on our boat *Maranatha*, on the few days we weren't cruising, we had dozed listlessly after lunch, emerging around five in the evening, unless we were lucky enough to be moored under trees.

When Jeff returned with the car, the boat was spit spot, and we headed off to the supermarket for a stock up. I had no intention of driving in Beziers, I was not fond of the car, we had sold mine when we sold our home and business and I drove it reluctantly, motors were fine but the one-way system in Beziers was not something a fancied tackling. The car park was situated underneath the shopping centre, and consequently deliciously cool. Whilst I went up and down in the lift several times until I identified the correct floor for the supermarket, The Husband remained in the car and had a snooze. The supermarket was within the shopping centre, and I was tempted to have a look around, but I knew that if I started shopping I would be hours and it had been a long day, plus my shorts and tee shirt were not really my image of sophisticated attire. After filling the car with lots of shopping, we loaded it on to the boat, unpacked and then went in search of a petrol station, we had used a lot of fuel since we left in March and wanted to top up with our containers. Three trips later we were done, and so was I. We locked the car up and hoped it would still be there, when we returned in a few days. An expensive day, and I didn't even buy any shoes! Later that evening, we received a telephone call, Jeff had dropped his mobile in the car park when he got out to help me with the shopping. We offered to come and collect it from the person who had found it, but they said we couldn't collect it for a few days. We didn't ever get the phone back, it was luckily a spare pay as you go phone. It seemed a little odd that the person that found it didn't hand the phone in the shopping centre, but took it home, perhaps they wanted a reward.

The next morning, we let the first batch of hire boats through the next lock, which was the second lock at Beziers, the hire boaters were all raring to go, and then took the second sitting. As there wasn't any proper mooring after the lock at Villeneuve les Beziers and the first lock at Beziers we knew that there wouldn't be many boats coming through, and as the locks were all controlled by lock keepers, no one nipping through before the correct opening time. The wind was quite strong and a bit of hesitance to avoid four hire boats exiting the lock sent us sideways, the port area is wide, and the easy course of action was to turn full circle and try again. The lock keeper obviously thought we had changed our minds so started to close the gates, we edged forwards and he reversed the command the gates reopened, and we entered the lock. The lock is over 6 meters deep, so the red-faced captain of *Jantina* had a few minutes to regain his composure as the water filled the lock. Not the best start to the day and later in the afternoon, we were due to tackle the 9 locks of Fonserrances, a staircase of 8 locks and 9 gates, another UNESCO site. There are not actually 9 locks functioning, as one of them links to the river, and is defunct, but they can hardly change the name.

Due to the number of locks, there is restrictive timings for entering the locks. We chose to tie up and walk to the lock and watch what fun the hire boaters had, whilst we established a technique for ourselves. The area around the locks has been developed into a tourist area with a drinks stall set up. Even at the early opening, the place was already mobbed but for once, the locks had barriers along some of it to stop people getting in the way. It looked like a day of being stared and pointed at, what fun! We had until 4.30 until we were due to go up so plenty of time to walk *Bilbo*. The waiting moorings were infinitely more pleasant than the port, and adjacent to a well-manicured park, which gave us the chance to avoid the sun and exercise *Bilbo*, whilst encountering a few other dogs on the way, we then returned to watch the 2.30 boats coming down, at some stage we would be returning, I hope not too soon, but a different technique would need to be employed so watching at leisure was helpful. Whilst we were walking back across the viaduct crossing the river Orb, I took few shots, including it seems some of our fellow tourists.

Beziers

When it was our time to leave, we cast off and took position in front of the first lock. When we had watched the hire boaters, as they normally had more than two on board, they were able to position themselves between each lock, those that didn't, walked from one lock to the next dragging the ropes up the steps. Each lock had a set of stone steps between them for this purpose. *Jantina,* sits much lower in the lock than hire boats and cruisers, so this but us at a disadvantage, but when we were in St Jean de Losne, we had purchased an extendable pole, it meant that in some instances, I didn't need to climb onto the salon roof to put a front rope on. In this instance, it was not long enough, due to each end of the lock having a straight piece, and the bollard set back from the edge, had I been the same height, I perhaps could have thrown a rope, but not with thirty onlookers. As we entered the lock, I climbed the ladder onto the roof, put the rope over the bollard, jumped down, ran to the back of the boat and then put the stern rope on my pole and handed it to the lock keeper. The stern of the boat had no such area for me to climb onto, and we had quickly realised that in order for me to get a rope on the back, which is derigeur on the Canal du Midi, it was necessary, to fold back a portion of the canopy, and leave the rope on the roof. I then needed to get off before the lock so that I could take the rope from Jeff with my pole and put it onto the bollard. We would implement this procedure for the next few weeks, until we left the Midi, as each lock had a waiting pontoon, specifically so you could get off and have a person on the shore to take ropes. The position of our canopy did not allow enough clearance to throw the rope, so it was the only thing we could do. After the first lock completed successfully, the pressure on Jeff to manoeuvre in and out of the lock professionally, as the hire boats were smashing from side to side, akin to the old 70's television programme, *It's a Knockout*. They all seemed to be having a hoot, whereas, if we hit the side, it was like driving into your own garage and our boat has the maneuverability of a shed on wheels so required some skill to complete all the locks without a scratch. Whilst Jeff showed off his steering skills, I was leaping around the boat like Wonder Woman. As the first lock had gone without a hitch, I then started running about, egged on by our audience, the lockkeeper stopped watching us after the second one and just walked over to take the rope. We made it through to the other side without a scratch, I felt like I had lost about half a stone during the time as the intense heat was taking its toll, as we exited, we got a round of applause, I bet we didn't even get on YouTube for that one, the only ever put the mess ups on!

We had now completed the last lock for 54 kilometres and were heading towards Columbiers, a small town with a hire boat harbour and small marina. A couple of years earlier we had stopped off in Columbiers on the way back from Spain. It was February and the weather was the bright sunshine that hints at the summer that is to come. Already the shoots were pushing through, we had left Spain with its orange blossom to drive back from the vineyards of the Languedoc and simply wanted to prolong the return to the frozen wastes of central France, and to commence working for the season at the lake.

Columbiers has a selection of chambre d hotes. We found out years ago, never stay in a hotel in France, always look for a chambre d'hote, hidden behind the shutters are the most delightful properties. Columbiers town has a series of winding roads, and the signs for the chambre de hotes at odd angles. We eventually came upon the rear of one. I tried the sensible option of ringing a telephone number to no avail and we sat in the car, staring at this idyllic property, blue shutters and magnolias trees, the French dream, I tried the bell, no response. I returned to the car and we were about to give up, when I spied someone walking across the lawn, quickly I dashed to the gate, and called

" Madame, Madame"

The lady came to the gate and I explained that we were looking to stay for a night. The chambre d'hôte was not due to open for another month, she and her husband were starting the outdoor work to get ready for the season. You would be forgiven in thinking that only boaters go to The Canal du Midi, but it is a tourist resort in its own right. Its position to so many places of historical interest appeal to some, the flora and fauna to others, cyclists, walkers, bird watchers and people like us, who just want some sun but not the hustle and bustle of a seaside resort. The property had a fabulous pool, and its gates at the far end of its garden opened onto the canal. We were shown into a splendid room and shown how to get to the garden room for breakfast in the morning.

After taking any valuables from the car and locking them in our room, we left them to their pruning and went for a stroll along the canal. We would probably never stay there, as the port was full, but we did take the number of the Captain's office, as to be expected, it all looked a little sad, the out of season resort feel. There was a main restaurant overlooking the port, which was closed but a small supermarket was open, as was a snack bar, and with the sunshine in abundance, the tables outside were full. A gorgeous building overlooked the canal, at the time I didn't realise it was also a hotel, but we had found our bed for the night, and most comfortable it looked, with a huge corner bath with a jacuzzi, what a treat after a long drive. Called *Au Lavoir*, I assume that at some stage it was converted from an old wash house, and a splendid job they had done of it. The menu didn't suit our tastes, or our pockets, we had just spent our second holiday in two months and needed to get back to earning some money, instead of spending it but that evening when we walked back into town, I wished that we had decided to go there, the building was lit up, the light dappling in the water of the canal, it was stunning. Instead, we went to the snack bar and had a pizza and a bottle of wine, which was extremely busy for February, but it was half term, in France, the reason we had managed to sneak away.

The following morning, after a delicious breakfast, cooked and served in the garden room, we said our farewells. The couple that owned it had retired from busy careers in Paris, to live a more tranquil life. Whilst we ate they chatted away to us, normally I would have found this annoying, but they were charming, and there story most interesting. Within ten minutes, we had called in to collect *Bilbo* from his frequent holiday home and the dog B and B in Beziers, and remarked to John and Ian, who are the proprietors and English, that *Au Lavoir*, appeared packed, for a Monday evening, the car park was full, and was told that the food was very good, which was why. It was the perfect end to our holiday, and with fond memories of Colombiers, on this occasion, we chugged along the canal hoping to stop nearby.

What we were met with was not such a warm welcome, it was late afternoon, and predictably, the moorings near to the town were all taken. What was a bit of a shock was, attached to all the houses along the canal, including our Chambre d Hote, were signs stating that mooring was prohibited. They certainly hadn't been there, when we visited before. Although, not legal, it was rather off putting to find yourself a pariah as you are in a boat. It appeared that the culling of the trees along the Canal

Du Midi, had created bad feeling and the locals resented the boaters, blaming them for damaging the trees. 42,000 plane trees were due to be felled along the Canal Du Midi, due to canker stain, a microscopic fungus, it's hardly surprising that there was some animosity. I believe that the boaters were being blamed for damaging the trees, perhaps they had, whether it was banging stakes into the roots of putting ropes around the trees, transmitting infection. It is a very distressing sight to observe the red crosses on the trees to be chopped down.

We advanced further through Columbiers, passed the signs to a suitable stop and I launched myself off onto the bank, taking a rope with me, this of course, would be the time when someone came cycling along the track, scowling because I had a rope across the track as was standing as far away from the edge to get a good pull on the rope. With one stake in, Jeff started to bang the next one in, and some dog walkers came along. I was shouting to tell him as their dogs were off the lead, we didn't want him to hit one of our furry friends. The dogs passed, and the owners got closer, stopping behind him as he yielded the sledge hammer, more shouting from me. I was beginning to wonder if we would ever get moored. It was after Seven when we finally got the rope tied up safely, we had employed the tactic of putting upturned plastic bottles onto the stakes so that people can see where they are, as we had found only a few days earlier, even if there is a clear towpath, for some reason people feel it is sensible to walk across the grass in front of a boat.

It had been a waring day, and rather disappointingly, was not going to be ended with a pizza, we were too far away to walk back, the food would be cold, and we certainly wouldn't be leaving the boat unattended, we may come back and find our ropes cut. As the evening drew on, more and more hire boats passed us, and joined us along both side of the banks, the sound of chatter in different languages and barbeques filling the air. In one week, we had been on two different canals, the Etang du Thau, and tackled the Nine Locks, I think it was about time for a rest. Tomorrow, we would try and moor in Capestang, where the desire to buy a canal boat had been born, I hope it doesn't disappoint.

Chapter Seven

You say Agave, I say Aloe Vera

The Languedoc conjures up imagines of sunflowers of Cyprus trees, lavender and sunflowers but so far on this journey we had seen little of any. We had mostly seen white hire boats, lots of churches and unusual locks. If it wasn't for the constant chirping of the cicadas, we could be have been, on any of the canal networks in France. Waking to the sunlight, shimmering on the water, we set off early, as without the restriction of the locks we could travel at our leisure. Three kilometres from Colombiers, sitting on the top of a hill is the Oppidum of Enserune, a pre-Roman fortified village and one of the first archaeological sites in Southern France. The museum displays remains of Greek, Celtic and Roman occupation. The canal du Midi passes under the foothills of the Oppidum through the tunnel of Malpas. Along the route there is also La Maison du Malpas, a cultural centre, with a bar to fortify yourself after the trek to the top, selling local wines to sample. As we passed along the section of the canal it was also possible to see a panoramic view of the Cevennes Mountains to Mount Canigou and the pond of Montady, which has a star shaped irrigation system, well it was possible for me, but not for

Jeff as he was steering and had to concentrate on not being hit by oncoming hireboats, whilst I pointed out what I could see and took photos.

After the tunnel of Malpas we approached the small village of Poilhes, always full of boats, but a very pretty secluded mooring, with a fabulous restaurant, so I have been informed. we couldn't have stopped anyway but we were on a mission, to Capestang. We had been trying to get a mooring at Capestang for years and on our way back from Spain, the previous winter, we had detoured to Capestang to the Captainaire, picked up the forms and posted them off to go on the waiting list for mooring. We had a mooring reserved on the Canal Tarn and Garonne but that was a further month's travel, and most importantly, not as good weather, should, by any miracle we had actual got a place we would stay put, the end of our travels over.

Although it was exceptionally early, we decided to moor up a way out of Capestang and walk into the village to establish if there was a space, suitable. We certainly didn't want to go passed and we couldn't turn around. We moored under some trees and prepared to walk along the canal. As we did so two blonde ladies came passed with three Jack Russell dogs and waved Hello to us. Taking *Bilbo* for a walk, we set off in the opposite direction to port and established that it was possible to moor along the bank, close to the port and returned to set about advancing along the canal. Although we knew the port well from visits by car, things change from year to year. Since our last visit, the tree culling had taken place and the shady bank of plane trees had gone, when we tried to moor two years later, in the same place that we moored, it had been converted into a mooring for bateau de plaisance/ hotel barges, so we were unable to stop, the quay as usual full of hire boats, as a base for the company *France Fluvial* and also the hire boat company *Hapimag*, plus electric boats it was hardly surprising the quay was packed. Plus, boats stopped for lunch, moored with no consideration to fellow boaters, leaving gaps between but not enough room for a boat. In this instance, we got our spot and proceeded to put stakes in, the two ladies and collection of dogs passed by again, *Bilbo* came out to say Hello, they then disappeared back to their respective boats.

Our mooring was perfect, with a bank above it, we were able to let *Matilda* out to explore, although she did spend a lot of time jumping back onto the boat when dogs passed by on the bank above. Sadly, with the trees gone there wasn't any shade, but on the plus side our solar panels were getting plenty of sun. At the top of some stone steps nearby we were treated to fabulous views of the Gothic Saint Etienne Church and of the whole village. If I had been in painting mode, it would have made a perfect picture, instead I had to be content to taking lots of photos. Above us was a very odd-looking plant, I would investigate exactly what it was at a later date.

That afternoon, we locked up and caught the bus to Beziers. I can't explain the novelty of being able to catch a bus anywhere. After years in France, where taxis were not taxis but ambulances or needed booking days in advance, to find a bus stop and the bus turn up, was nothing short of miraculous. A few years ago, we had stayed in the town of Prades for a few days. We had set off with the intention of going to watch the testing of the new Formula one cars for the year at Barcelona, dropped *Bilbo* off in Beziers, then decided the weather was grotty in Barcelona, so sitting around for three days hoping to catch a glimpse of Lewis Hamilton, whilst it drizzled continuously did not appeal. Instead we decided to spend a few days exploring the Pyrenees. As we drove there we were astounded to see lots of buses, with banners 1€ Return to Perpignan. Had we wanted to go to Perpignan would we have been enticed to hop on, but I had quickly booked us into the most fantastic Chambre de Hote in a converted villa in the centre of the town. It was February, and we had a huge balcony with a view of Mount Canigou. The same Mountain that we would view from the boat on the way to Capestang. The trip proved a success, despite meeting up with snow ploughs on the way up the mountain and me being scared witless. To view the mountain from the canal, and know you have been to the top of it is rather satisfying, we do sight see, just not much on the boat. The buses had stuck in my mind, and here we were, lined up at the bus stop in the village of Capestang, it was most surreal.

The bus turned up, and on time, and we were dropped off at the train station, just a hop, skip and a jump from the port, where we had left it the day before. The bus quickly filled with passengers, and as the heat exceeded thirty-eight degrees, the driver switched the air conditioning on full blast, which was a blessed relief. Within five minutes, we heard shouting from a young man. He asked her to switch it off as he was too cold. She refused, and he grew agitated, walking up and down the aisle, shouting, she threatened to evict him several times, meanwhile, several girls had decided to film him shouting, on their phones, this antagonised him further. The female bus driver, viewing this from her mirror, slowed down at the next stop and forced him to disembark. He certainly would miss the air conditioning now! We recouped our car, tyres intact and drove back to Capestang, delighted at the efficient service, and impressed at how the driver dealt with him. I was also impressed that for not much money, I could escape from the boat, should I so desire, for some retail therapy, or culture, if the mood took me. This day was getting better and better.

Settled back at the boat, *Bilbo* walked, I put a post on Facebook *'Hurrah, have arrived in Capestang, finally'*. A few hours later, I received a response. *"Where are you moored I'll pop down and see you?"*

 Earlier that Spring, when we had called in to put our names on the waiting list for the port, afterwards we had taken a stroll along the canal. Moored up was a beautiful old boat, similar to ours, with the wing shaped lee boards. The couple that owned it were onboard, and in the middle of some serious varnishing when we passed. We had made an admiring comment and ended up chatting to them. They told us that regretfully, they no longer lived aboard as their daughter, who then popped her head out to see who they were talking to, had started school in the village. They were no longer able to live the fluid lifestyle required for boating and the boat was up for sale. It was Jane, from that boat, who knocked on our door later that day. After a quick catch up, we were invited round for a drink to their home, later in the week. Even *Bilbo* was invited. It was Jane that I asked first about the strange tree near to us, she informed me it was Aloe Vera.

The following day, we realised that by ten it was too hot to go outside, *Bilbo* was used to walking early, but without a day's cruising we were at odds with what to do with ourselves. Jeff decided to touch up some of the paint that understandably had been knocked off on the way. On the outskirts of the village, adjacent to the supermarket was its sister company, Bricomarche. We would become regular visitors during our stay. Having walked around the village the previous day, looking for the bus stop, I had little desire to trek back in the heat and was grateful for the car, with air conditioning, in fact, while it was near, we took every opportunity to avail ourselves of the cool interior. It wasn't that I didn't appreciate waking every morning to the Azure Blue sky, but in the middle of France, there was some respite from the heat, usually after three days of heat a thunderstorm and rain, and the heat would break a little. In the Languedoc, the air felt as though a hair dryer was blowing all day, the wind originating from North Africa, blew fine sand particles in the air, not ideal for painting, and not too good on the windows either, along with the bugs, on our side of the bank, without any shelter, I was being to feel as though we were in the Sahara.

One of the consequences of the heat, was that only the foolish, were on deck during the day, I would nip *Bilbo* outside for a quick wee and then back inside. Since we had arrived in Avignon, our television reception had become almost non-existent, when we were moving it didn't really matter and we were aware it would be problem the further South we went. I had notice that one of the boats had an abnormally large satellite dish, so I decided to take action and ask the owners if it worked to pick up Uk television, it was the British Grand Prix at Silverstone the following weekend, so if we could find a solution by then, I would have a happy husband. The boat belonged to one of the blonde ladies with the Jack Russell's and her husband. She was outside, on the deck, when I posed the question, and she suggested we came around for drinks that evening and they could tell us what to do.

The couple Trish and Freddy were great company and invited us to stay for a barbeque, joining them were their two doggies, *Clara* and *Jackson*, I always enjoy an evening onboard with dog owners as they provide additional entertainment, you don't ever quite know what they will do. Doggie diversions were not necessary that evening, as the conversation flowed, and we invited them for dinner later in the week. During the evening, we mentioned that we were 'on the list' for mooring, and they told us that the Captain we had left, and the new one had taken over that week, and to go and see her. Nursing a hangover, the following morning, I joined Trish and the other lady Kate, for their morning walk. She seemed totally unaffected, whereas I felt more than ropey. *Bilbo* was overjoyed, he now had three little buddies to play with, *Clara, Jackson* and *Boris*. For once I left him off the lead as the walk took us into through some fields, with only the canal on the other side he was safe, and hopefully didn't have anywhere he could run off to, which was his usual behaviour. Once I returned, I walked round to the Tourist office, where the Captain's office was situated on the opposite side of the quay. I was impressed that she knew exactly where we were moored, she was obviously on the ball. I know we aren't exactly small, but we were in the 'free' part on a bank and enquired to our winter mooring. She told me that she wouldn't know if we had a place until September, but our application was not in the file and gave me a new application form to complete. Her advice was, if we had anywhere else to go then we should, as it was unlikely we would have a space for the winter. As we walked back round, Trish and Freddy were on their deck and enquired who we had got on. I explained, and they suggested we stayed in port and we were more likely to get a space if we were there. We were undecided, if we left port, we could turn around and come back as winter mooring doesn't commence until November. It was a difficult choice, we could spend the rest of the summer in Capestang with these friendly people, two hours' drive closer to Spain, where we were going to spend the winter, in our caravan. The weather was infinity better in Capestang than Moissac, where we had a reservation but the Captain there, had been extremely helpful, and our friends Sally and Glenn were booked in for the winter. We were in a quandary, and we weren't the only one. When you buy a boat, you are advised to make sure you have a mooring, it is not easy but not impossible in France, but you may not be somewhere you want to be. When you set off at the beginning of the year, some people have no idea where they will be by the end of the season, as it is impossible to predict ahead, but many boaters in France do not live aboard, or travel that far, therefore it is essential to have the reassurance of a guaranteed mooring. We put this decision on the back burner, we were not in rush to leave, it was nice that Trish and Freddy wanted us to stay but they had a house, nearby, so they wouldn't be onboard over the winter. Kate and her husband, after years in Capestang, were leaving and Jane had told us that their boat had been broken into that winter, when the boat was locked up and they were at home. Despite daily dog walks and runs along the canal, and plenty of friends nearby they had still fallen victim. We would not be onboard either, so the boat would be more vunerable to theft.

To add to our consideration, the gendarmes knocked on our door with a leaflet, advising us of thefts in the area, and urging us to be vigilant happens everywhere, as we have first-hand experience, with our first house broken into, and our lake buildings three times we were alarmed but certainly not naïve to think we were unsusceptible At least the gendarmes were being proactive. In holiday mode it's easy to be lapse. We made sure that even if we went or a walk the boat was double locked and alarmed, checking all the windows were locked scrupulously.

Jeff started painting early that evening, whilst I took *Bilbo* out, once the sun had gone down. He was hopping off the boat to assist hire-boaters moor, taking a rope something he had been doing since we stopped. From a private boat came a grumpy man, and admonished my husband for assisting them. Some people are so miserable, the first to complain if the inexperienced boaters cause damage, we were trying to get them moored up and off the water quickly as the volume of traffic coming through the port exceeded the spaces available and if they were lingering mid water caused further drama. Tomorrow they will be gone to crash and bang in another port and a new selection of boats and its occupants would arrive, to search for bread in the village and take photos of the church.

We decided to take a trip to Cap D'Agde, we still needed to get to a marina, when you have a boat there are always things you need to buy. We were about forty-five minutes away, and the journey took us back along the Canal Du Midi as Cap D'Agde is the seaside resort of Agde, where we had encountered the Round lock, a week or so earlier. Cap D'Agde is one of the largest seaside resorts in the South of France, on the Med. Since the Sixties, it has been a naturist resort, and has been so popular with the Germans, wishing to bare their flesh in a warm environment, they even set up a post box in the town, going direct to Germany. All we wanted for some rope, not to be used in the naughty way, we had broken three ropes in our first lock at the beginning of the year, although I am sure the chandlers would have had some interesting requests over the years, particularly as, I discovered whilst researching the area on the internet is a big area for swingers and porn. As I have commented before, sometimes it's better to be naïve.

Much more our sort of thing, between Cap d' Agde and Agde is a former volcano, the Mont Saint Loup. Rising to 113 m covering 15 km. It erupted 750,000 years ago and gave Agde its grey colour and basalt monuments. Carved into the coastline and creating fabulous landscape. A view that is food for the soul.

We arrived in Cap D' Agde, the built -up holiday resort on the sparkling sea, fortunately, we managed to keep our clothes on, as we actual needed to be in the Zone Technique, which was situated in the shipyard at Cap D' Agde, full of gin palaces, some in the water, others on blocks. We doubted whether we would find what we were looking for, our eighteen strand yellow barge ropes were probably not a requirement on something you were more likely to see in Monaco. The staff at the chandlers were helpful, one spoke English, I suppose with boats of all nationalities moored there it was essential to have a member of staff that could communicate. It was also something we had noticed, since travelling further South, that more people spoke English but that was logical, we had been the only English family living in our region, there is a mix of Brits, Dutch and Germans settled in the South, all seeking a greater life in the sun.

We left with four ropes, our assistant assuring us they would be strong enough for the locks, Jeff and I both fighting with our instincts to buy things that we didn't need. We wanted to buy some fenders, but the brilliant white ones on offer would look a bit silly on our green and cream paintwork. They were aimed at the lookalike white boats for the Med, at least we had got some new ropes, you don't know what catastrophe is around the corner. The drive back, we passed vineyard after vineyard, it truly is a beautiful region, and with the coast so close by, it is easy to see how people fall in love with the area, and never want to leave.

That evening, we went to Jane and John's for drinks, the couple that had been staining the wood on their barge back in the Spring. It was evident they had put many hours into creating a stunning home. From handmade tiles in the cloakroom, donated by a boating friend, to the renovated floor tiles, the property was unique and utterly gorgeous. I could have given up my boat to live there, at the drop of a hat. It reminded me a little of our first house in France, that I fell in love with as I walked across the threshold and as we sat in the courtyard looking at the flowers from the properties above I could have been transported back to our old home. *Dickson*, their dog, welcomed *Bilbo*, which is always surprising when a new dog enters their home, and their daughter happily splashed in the paddling pool, then came and sat with us, making us special cards.

It was an idyllic evening, the sort we had shared many times in our old home, the stars twinkling above in the night sky, the summer heat making the night endless but usually an evening like that is shared with long-time friends, not new acquaintances, but Jane and I had led parallel lives, the same age, moving to and from the same places, a bizarre coincidence, I felt like I had known her all my life. Their daughter, initially wary of these strangers in her house, chattered away, and although our daughter was now a 'grown up' allegedly, it seemed like only yesterday we were having the same conversations. As our daughter had been at French school, I suppose we understood more of her life than the usual English visitors, although I think her French was a little better than ours. Despite drinking copious amounts of the superb wine from the local Cooperative, we walked through the narrow winding streets on a high, rather than drunkenly, listening to the chatter of people still awake in their gardens.

Not wanting to stop their adventures completely, Jane and John had purchased an antique turquoise Citroen van, which they affectionately called' Hettie'. They were worked furiously to get Hettie in a good state to allow them to take a camping trip after Bastille Day, as part of the local community essential to stay for the celebrations, but also because their daughter's birthday was that week. So rather a lot to get done in a week. The van was a work in progress, but they had fitted a mini kitchen, I think tents would be employed for sleeping, it was adorable, and very then, it made our newly purchased caravan look nasty in comparison. The shaped of the house allowed a workshop in the courtyard, our similar property had a kitchen in the same space and a utility room on the other side. Thank goodness, we hadn't seen this house before we sold up, otherwise we may have had some restructuring occurring. The workshop housed lots of tools. Jane had recently started a business making things out of old wine casks, called *Barrel Boutique*. Ideally suited to commissions, working around the school hours. The local Tourist office sold the products there, but now she has an online shop and is very busy, the commissions growing larger by the day. When I first met Jeff, he had a tool room set up in the conservatory in his house, and later as the business expanded we had industrial units full of tools. Some girls do not get excited at pillar drills and sanders, I do, although truthfully, using them I am not so good at, but I love tools. Jane showed me what she was currently making, the pungent smell of sawdust filling my nostrils. I felt privileged to see this centre of industry, an artisan at work. Now when I see pictures of her commissions, I can picture her working away in her workshop, dungarees on, surrounded by wood shavings, isn't that what we all crave, to be our master of our own destiny and certainly doing it in the South of France, holds more appeal than Macclesfield for example.

The rest of the week, John would pass in the evening with *Dickson* and one or both of us would walk *Bilbo*. That dog was having such a great time and Jeff had the opportunity to chat with someone with more worldly views than mine, regaling him with sailing stories and suggestions of how to convert our stupid caravan to hot water, as we had been duped by the salesman when we bought it.

It was our turn to host, Trish and Freddy were coming for dinner, food prepared I strolled into the village for some bread and noticed one of the boutiques open. For someone that seems to have far too many clothes for a person living on a boat, I seemed to be running out of outfits to wear in the evening. The problem with staying in one place, people will think you have the same clothes on, most of my wardrobe consisted of stripy tops and shorts, my summer clothes that I would have worn when we lived in town not suited an evening onboard, and I had worn all my casual evening clothes since we arrived. I had got rid of all my summer dresses and kept some flippy skirts and tops. The lure of something new appealed, but after stripping off in the unairconditioned shop, I realised I was far too hot to be trying clothes on grabbed a loose bright blue tunic, it came with a thin vest top, but it was evidently aimed at a ten-year-old as it certainly didn't reach my waist, perhaps it was a crop top for ladies with long boobs. I got changed for dinner and Jeff commented that you could see through my tunic, lacking the energy for a search for a suitable undergarment, I abandoned it and put something else on. I really needed to go shopping if we were going to stay in the South.

It's amazing how you can different people bring out different behaviour in people. Freddy reminded me of the friends that Jeff had when we first met many moons ago and they had fallen into an immediate rapport, teasing each other mercilessly, perhaps it's because they both came from seaside towns, but it was strange, to see a glimpse of the husband I had first fallen for. It's a good job it was only for an evening though because he (Jeff) was a nightmare, only the responsibility of our daughter had made him grow up. Thank goodness, we were in a sleepy French village, we had a great evening, Trish had travelled a lot before she settled down and I was fascinated by her story, but with two dominate males in the room, I would have to wait until a walk before she could get a word in edgeways. It's rare to find two couples where they are all very talkative, but we all had so many stories to share. What I did managed to find out from them, was that the plant was Agave. The verdict is still out on that one.

Friday evening, the old captain, was hosting a karaoke night, at the bar in the village. We had intended to go, but three nights drinking in a week was beginning to take its toll, combined with the relentless heat, we cried off, which was probably for the best, but a shame as we would have had a chance to meet more of the locals. When we were due to go out, Jeff had a second wind and decided to get on with some painting whilst it was a big cooler. It was probably a good thing as I don't think my liver would have taken it. Jeff was obviously not recovered totally, as when he finished painting, he leaned on the table, and bent it, good job we hadn't guests that evening.

On Saturday morning, I got ready to catch the bus into Beziers, my favourite sandals had broken, my spare pair I had split nail polish all over in Spain in the winter, so it was time for some new ones. Jane had been wearing some floaty palazzo pants I was taken with and I quite fancied a new floaty top, as I had ripped the sleeve on my favourite, climbing off our old boat *Beau*, after one too many glasses of wine the previous autumn. As I walked passed Trish and Freddie's boat, they asked me where I was going, all dressed up, I literally had a dress on, not my usual boating attire. When I explained I was going into Beziers shopping, they told me that they were on their way home, and they would drop me off in Beziers, if I wanted a lift. Accepting their offer, I followed them to the car and when we approached Beziers, they dropped me off, at what was obviously the centre, but I had no idea where I was. I wanted to go to the Octogen Centre, which was not far from the canal. I was in the historic centre, on the other side of town. I got my wish to see the more traditional side of Beziers, but by the time I got to the shopping centre, I was shattered.

I used to be the sort of person that could spend a day shopping, now I lack the enthusiasm for leisurely browsing. Perhaps I have been spoilt from shopping in Vitry le Francois, where I will buy a seasons clothes in one shop. I lack the patience to wander aimlessly from shop to shop. At an advantage, as I know the brands I like, I went straight to *Andre*, the shoe shop that the last pair had come from, then dithered as to whether I should buy red or black but chose red as black is boring and then went in search of the floaty trousers. I wasn't entirely convinced but I bought a pair, with the colour of my new top in the pattern, okay, time to go.

I made my way to the train station, where we had been dropped off by the bus earlier that week and searched for the bus stop. Up and down I walked but I could not find a bus to go to Capestang. I asked people waiting, I asked bus drivers, no one could tell me what number bus I wanted or where to wait. Giving up, I then telephoned Jeff to ask him to collect me, but the battery was flat, and it had switched off. It all seemed so simple when I set off this morning. Exasperated, I decided I would have to get a taxi back to Capestang, goodness knows what it would cost. Standing at the taxi rank, there weren't any cars arriving, I was beginning to think I wouldn't ever get back, as it had taken me a lot longer to get to the shopping centre than anticipated, I had expected to be back by lunchtime and knew that Jeff would start to be concerned something had happened. I am a big girl, but my husband does fret that something will happen to me. I found a number of a taxi company and rang them, it would a twenty-minute wait. I had little option but to wait, and finally the taxi came and dropped me in the village. My mornings shopping had proved very expensive, I wished I had driven now. That evening, we had an early evening drink at the restaurant on the quay, we had eaten there many years ago, stopping off for lunch on the way back from the Monaco Grand Prix, the restaurant had been taken over since then, the menu not so appealing to us. It was pleasant having a beer and watching the boats go by, but we had more shade on our boats deck, than sitting outside the restaurant, and the drinks were cheaper!

As Bastille Day was the following week, there was a big fuss happening in port. The boats in the paying part all had to move, there was going to be a huge firework display, which would be taking part on the bridge above the lock. The bridge at Capestang is famous amongst boaters as it is the lowest on the Canal Du Midi and many a boat has come a cropper navigating it. We had that fun to encounter when we left. It was not necessary to move until the day, but some boats were leaving before the event, including Kate and Mark, with their little dog *Boris*. As Trish and Freddy were at home for the weekend, Kate called for me on the way for her dog walk, *Bilbo* was a little confused as to where Jackson and Clara were, but enjoyed someone to one to one playing with *Boris*. We walked up to say goodbye on Monday morning and *Bilbo* sat patiently waiting for *Boris*, he was going to miss all his Capestang friends when we left. Boris was also a frequent visitor to the dog B and B and I wondered if they should ever be there together, would they remember their summer friendship.

On Tuesday, Freddy returned without Trish, the air conditioning on the boat had stopped working so she had made the sensible decision to remain at home with the dogs by her swimming pool. I wish I could have gone there too. That afternoon, the bank near us became full as the boats left the quay and came passed the first bridge, the point of safety according to the local pompiers. We were fine where we were moored as we were far enough away, which was convenient as the last touch of paint was being applied in, so we didn't really want to move.

Next to us, pulled up a British registered narrowboat, the occupant was obviously a Capestang regular, as the locals came to welcome him. That evening, we were serenaded by the sounds from his bag pipes! Strangely, the Tourist boat arrived from Villeneuve les Beziers and moored in the middle of the quay that had been evacuated, evidently the fire restrictions didn't apply to them! As the excitement for the Bastille celebrations built up, we were at a bit of a loss. With the restaurant fully booked for the evening, we weren't keen to go into the village and leave the boat unattended. The warnings from the gendarmes fresh in our minds, if ever there was an opportunity for some thieving, it was on a night with lots of strangers wandering around in the dark. We made the decision to carry on with our journey along the Canal du Midi, we were torn as we were settled there, but we didn't buy a boat to stay in one spot and we knew we would be frustrated after a couple of weeks if we stayed.

We had finished our painting and decided we needed to buy a rug for our lounge and with Beziers only a short drive away we headed off to one of the furniture shops on the outskirts of the town. Beziers is forever busy and there seems to have been road works there for the last five years, so we got horrendously lost, our sat nav sending us in circles as we kept meeting a dead end as the road was blocked off. It did give us the chance to drive round in the cool and see some of the villages that we wouldn't find along the canal. More wine, more olives and more interesting buildings. We also decided to take a drive back to Cap D'Agde, for something else we needed, but whatever it was they didn't have, and we decided to drive to the nearby fishing port of Grau d' Agde to have a look in the chandlery there. Grau was charming, a picturesque seaside town, with candy coloured holiday cottages and little boat bobbing on the sea. The streets were packed with families carry the days necessities to the beach. We found the chandleries easily and stopped for coffee before heading back empty handed. We would wait until we were moored somewhere for a while and rely on Poste Restante to get what we needed delivered to the post office.

Our last night in Capestang was Bastille night, I had bought a card to activate the water from the Captain, and we intended on leaving first thing, before the boats came into port, allowing us to tie up on an empty quay, fill up with water and go. The second reason for going then, was that we were concerned about passing through the low bridge. Jeff had attached fenders along our roof line, the horse shoe shaped most likely to scrape the sides or the top of the roof. We had been in a quandary, as we needed to get water, but the more we put in, the higher the level of the boat, so we were effectively going to make our boat rise in the water, closer to the bridge. The earlier we left, the better chance we had of making a clear run at the bridge.

The morning of Bastille Day, announcements were made through the tannoy system for the church. We woke to the sounds of the *La Marseillaise*, the French National Anthem. Throughout the day music played interspersed with announcements, by early evening, a concert was taking place. As the light began to dim, hordes of people set off walking along the path above the canal, small children stumbling in the dark over ropes, when their stupid parents decided to try and cut through the crowds to get a better position to see the display. We took some cushions to the front of the boat, and sat on our lounge roof to get a good view, the pets inside. As the last firework exploded, the crowds dispersed, and we climbed down to go inside, our last night in Capestang, under the velvet sky, the smell of gunpowder filling the air.

Waking to another cloudless sky, we quietly set off into the port. Much to my amazement, Karen the new Captain, was already working, she had taken over on the busiest week of the year and the adrenalin was obviously keeping her going as she was 'on duty' until gone midnight, the night before. We had left with her a completed form for the following winter, the best solution. Circumstances change, and Karen now is in charge of the hire boats for Hapimag, based in Capestang. As we finished filling up, one of the boats that normally resided along the quay arrived and we stopped to help them, then finally got on our way around Eight am, just before the first hire boat came through the bridge, but with care, as it was being driven by one of the staff, the boats for hire all needed to go back to their positions, it was going to be a busy morning in port. To my relief we got through the bridge without any drama, and started on the next leg of our journey, new places to see, new friends to make.

Chapter Eight

Mad Cats and Ginger Ones

After lunch we arrived in the small village of Argeliers, without any locks along this stretch of the canal, it was an easy day, for me anyway as I wasn't at the helm, not so much for Jeff as every corner twists and turns like a snake. The next day we were due to arrive in Le Somail, and I hoped desperately, we would find somewhere to moor. Prunella Scales and Timothy West had made a series of programmes for Channel Four in England, called' Great Canal Journeys', several episodes featured France, and one the Canal du Midi. On the programme, they had stopped at Le Somail and visited a bookshop. We would have to wait until tomorrow to find out if we could visit it. There was little to report, except that Argeliers had a restaurant, 'Le chat qui Peche', which understandably was closed, having probably taken a week's turnover in a night, the previous evening. I was happy that our cat *Matilda*, could wander without being chased by dogs, but hoped she didn't fancy a spot of fishing.

Refreshed from stopping early in Argeliers, we made an early start hoping to get a spot on the quay. When we arrived at Le Somail, we realised that there weren't any spots on the quay, the shots on the programme in front of an enchanting restaurant and chambre de hote situated overlooking the canal, wisteria climbing, did not include a hotel barge moored directly in front of it. The rest of the quay was taken up with a hotpotch of boats that obviously are permanent and various hire boats. Le Somail is the hire boat base of *Minervois Cruisers*, which have cute narrow boats, which in fact Pru and Tim, were using during that part of their journey. Further along is another hire boat base, for the company Nichols and a tourist office.

We sailed passed and determined to have my day, we moored on the bank, back to scrambling about with stakes and sledgehammers. Once we were tied up, we took *Bilbo* for a stroll and looked around. The harbour was as pretty as it had looked on the television, with a Museum and wine tasting on the quay and we quickly found the antiquarian bookshop. It only took about ten minutes to walk around and on our way back I noticed a boat shop, something which I gather is quite common in England, but very unusual in France. I checked the hours of opening to return later, without *Bilbo* and with some cash, I didn't really need to buy anything, but if you don't support the local businesses then next time, when you come, they won't be there.

Stupidly, I had not thought the bookshop would only sell French books, but browsing in the two rooms, the smell of old books, it would be easy to get carried away and forget and buy a French book, but my language skills are really not up to reading anything more than a magazine advert or the back of a packet for cooking instructions. It was an interesting diversion, and the painted heads of some favourite authors were there but as they were French I would not have recognised any of them. I suspect that they did little tourist trade as antique books are not what a boat full of children desire.

The boat shop was a more successful visit, selling home made products as well as some tourist items, all at extortionist prices, but then I don't' expect the mooring rates for their barge are a bargain either. As the tourist office was open, I popped it to ask if there was a train station or bus stop nearby, as we had the rest of the day free we could collect the car. It seemed that this part of the Canal du Midi did not run near a train and there wasn't a stop for the bus, so we returned to the boat and enjoyed an afternoon off. Later in the afternoon, we walked back to the restaurant and enjoyed a drink on the bustling terrace, we wouldn't be dining there like Tim and Pru, but we could try the local wine and soak in the atmosphere. The following day we would be back to the fun of the locks, I was not looking forward to it.

We set off for the day and because the locks were assisted by lock keepers, we had to stop for lunch. It is not something that we would normally do, preferring to make an early start, when it is cooler, then stop mid-afternoon. We had little option to stop at lunch time and tie up along the bank. As Noel Coward said' *Only mad dogs and Englishmen go out in the midday sun'* Well our dog was not mad, and this English lady had no desire to expose herself to the full force of the sun every day, but as we were obligated to stop, I would find myself every day on the tow path, with a reluctant *Bilbo,* trying to find some shade to walk in. I had taken to spraying him with sunscreen, as he was pink parts and his black hair is permanently faded in parts due to a life in sunny France. The other problem with stopping at lunchtime is, by 1.30, when you were supposed be sitting outside the lock raring to go, there would be a queue of boats behind you, all vying for the next lock, and obviously the same on either side, it would be up to the lock keeper to decide you goes first and sometimes, you would have a long wait, as the lock behind you would open, and the next set of plastic tubs would come at you.

With little on the itinerary that day, we left one mooring after a lock and moored for the night, further along the canal in a similar mooring, with nothing but trees and fields, and locks obviously. With the Canal Du Midi cycle route running next to the tow path, *Matilda* had to make a sharp exit to the other side of the tow path and sit under the trees, watching for the next batch of lunatics, thinking they were doing the Tour de France. Occasionally, on our journey, we would see a lone man or woman with a trailer and their worldly possessions packed up, sometimes, there may be a dog in the trailer, other times not, and occasionally we would see them set up in tents along the tow path. As well as ducks and boaters there is lots of life along the towpath.

Our last day before the weekend, when we try to avoid cruising due to the new hire boaters, and the rush of those completing their holiday, racing to get back to port. We kept our day reasonably short stopping before a double lock at a place called Ognon. It was a perfect mooring, tucked out of the way from the lock, underneath the trees, and without the need for acrobatics as it had mooring posts. It was mid-afternoon and a restaurant /bar across the other side of the canal had a sign outside for ice-creams, so our dog walk could have a treat at the end of it. As we were on the side of the canal without the towpath beside it, it meant we would be undisturbed by a constant stream of cyclists and walkers, stopping and staring at our boat, the only one it seemed moving that wasn't white or plastic! As a hotel barge approached the lock, we decided to walk *Bilbo* so that we could watch how they did it, and also to see how quickly the locks filled and emptied for the next day. The boat went into the lock effortlessly, its sun canopy lowering, rather like the electric roof of sports car and whilst the lock was filling a lady lay on a sunlounger, reading a book, totally disinterested in the experience. As most hotel barges, actually don't go very far, they don't go through that many locks during the course of the holiday, and we would have expected some degree of interest, usually the passengers watch what is happening, as every lock is different, surely that is part of the entertainment. It was a secluded spot, and for once no one except us was watching. I did notice that the lady was wearing high heels with her long floaty dress and was horrified that she had worn such footwear on the beautiful teak deck. The boat departed the two locks and the mechanised canopy returned to its position shielding her from the sun, the only thing that she seemed slightly interested in.

We walked back, and were disappointed to discover that the Auberge, did indeed serve ice creams, but not at 4 in the afternoon. The tables were laid up for the evening sitting and the owners were obviously having a break. We returned to the boat and let *Matilda* out. With some woods behind the mooring and a small country lane leading to a farm, the only buildings she was relatively safe, or so we thought. I had gone inside to find refreshment and *Bilbo* was laying on the deck in the shade, when suddenly we heard an almighty scream and *Matilda* flew back onto the boat, and through the double doors into the boat. A large tom cat was outside the boat and had obviously taken a shine to our three-legged lady. We took *Bilbo* outside onto the hardstanding of the mooring, thinking that this would deter the cat. It then ran up a tree. Jeff took a chair outside and sat with *Bilbo* and *Matilda*, evidently feeling protected by Jeff and the dog, bravely ventured back outside, at which the cat then jumped down from the tree and chased her again. We decided that we would put her inside as we were concerned she would run off into the thicket. The cat then tried to get through the roof hatches. We proceeded to close every window to keep the nuisance out, it was a thing possessed. Giving up on getting in, it returned to the tree for a few hours and we sat on the deck after dinner watching it and the cars arriving at the restaurant opposite. It seemed that well dressed and the affluent of the area, were dining in the Auberge opposite, as every car that arrived was an expensive one, which is rare to see in France, unless you are in Nice, as it is not encouraged to flash your wealth, as the tax man cometh! That's obviously why they didn't need to open to sell an odd ice-cream to a passing tourist.

We went to bed and forgot about the cat, and the next morning, Jeff took *Bilbo* for a walk whilst I was tidying up after breakfast, the wait for the lock keeper at 9 am giving us more time than usual in the morning. *Matilda* had hopped off the boat when Jeff and *Bilbo* had gone out and I hadn't taken much notice, as normally Jeff would let her out and then look for her when I returned with *Bilbo*, but our routine was all at sea. Suddenly I heard a screech, and a splash, I ran outside, and *Matilda* was in the canal grappling at the sides of the boat to get back on. Quickly, I ran inside and grabbed the landing net, a giant net for fishing and scooped her out. We kept it in the wheelhouse at all time, in case this ever happened. Wet and distressed, she limped off into the lounge and when Jeff returned with *Bilbo* I had her bundled in my arms like a baby, wrapped in a towel. The cat stayed on the side of the quay, doubtless waiting for its net victim to terrorise.

Our next day took us to Homps, a small village with several restaurants a village shop and another hire boat base. Le Boat. We had stopped off at Homps before in the car and I my impression was that it was tatty, but looking at anywhere out of season doesn't shed it in the best light. Our old insurance agent Cyrille, had told us to go to the restaurant at Homps as it was owned by his cousin, but there was more than one and we could hardly go and ask them all if they were owned by Cyrille's cousin, although I am sure we would have received good treatment if we had. We followed the same trick as normal mooring up before the town and walking up to see if there was any space. There was a big gap right on the quay, so we hurried to get into the space before someone else did and successfully moored, then we realised why it perhaps was vacant. It was right next to the dustbins. The smell was rancid, and we quickly closed the fly screens. *Matilda* would not be going out as we were on a quay in a busy spot, but I doubt whether she would be too enthusiastic after the mornings antics.

Taking a stroll to the local shop, after purchasing a few items, I enquired if the owner was aware of a taxi company in the area. She was extremely helpful and telephone someone and arranged for someone to pick us up in half an hour. We locked the boat up and he drove us to Capestang, it was not a cheap ride, Fifty Euros, so we wouldn't be dining out that evening. With the car back, we called into the supermarket and stocked up again, after a few days living on pasta, quick fixes in a hot kitchen at the end of a hot day, I was looking forward to cooking my favourite

Gambas, bought from the fresh fish counter. We may not be dining out, but we would be dining in style.

The port at Homps is a mix of styles, further along from the quay, walking away from the town is a wine boutique with the obligatory tasting an option, boats line either side of the canal and a chambre de hote is tucked away along the track to the next lock. An unusual piece of metalwork, a large blue spiral shaped bridge crosses the canal, giving access to another Le Boat hire base with an area for motor homes behind it. On the side opposite the port has a selection of houses, and a less formal restaurant, the area further along not so well manicured, which was odd as the area reserved for hotel barges was on the less desirable side.

On the side we were moored, with our lovely smell, a few spaces for overnight stops and a smattering of boats permanently moored, including a day cruise boat, a pirate boat and a chapel boat. It didn't see anyone on the chapel boat, but the hours of service were posted on a blackboard outside. As we would be leaving on Sunday morning, I would not get to see if it was in use, but I was intrigued as to whether it was a permanent fixture or moved along the canal giving sermons.

In the evening I cooked a lovely dinner of prawns, with sauté potatoes and salad and we ate on the deck, enjoying our Saturday evening, it is unusual for restaurants in France to have music playing on the terrace and the gentle chatter could be heard from the restaurants on either side of the quay. A hire boat had managed to squeeze in behind the hotel barge that we had seen the day before in the lock. It was so close to the boat was almost touching. The guests on the hotel barge were being served their dinner by the crew when the German teenager on the hire boat started to play his guitar. Once he had got into the swing of things he accompanied his playing with singing. His chosen song was one of Ed Sheeran's' he wasn't bad it became evident that it was the only song that he knew, by the third time, we heard him play it, Jeff suggested I played a cd, so we couldn't hear him. The people on the hotel barge, did not look amused at their free entertainment, it was like being moored next to a busker, with limited repartee.

We set off the following morning, leaving the smell and flies behind, and our car parked on the quay, we hopefully could get a bus back for the next move. As we were waiting for the first lock at the stopping place before it a hire boat pulled up with a French couple. They had come straight from the port after collecting the boat and were unsure what to do. We told them that we would travel with them for the next few locks if they wanted us to and Jeff gave them a few pointers. For once, she had sensible shoes on for boating, instead of the usual flip flops that people seem to think are a good idea running around on a boat with little experience and ropes dangling. We did three locks with them and when we stopped for lunch, they were more confident to set off for the afternoon. As we waited at one of the locks, I noticed loads of fenders on the side, we were building up a collection of broken fenders, after slicing a few open trying to moor on the waiting pontoons, the metal spikes seeming to slice nicely into our rubber protectors. As we were waiting for the other boats to tie up I asked the lock keeper what they were for, and she told me, that they fished them out of the locks every day, so anyone could take them as they always had lots. So, we took two, and she let me put the broken ones in the bin, what a nice girl! They weren't as smart as ours but needs must.

We approached a waiting pontoon for a double lock at l'Aiguille and tied up to wait, then large three hire boats and a small sailing boat arrived. As the other boats would fill the lock, I walked up to the lock to speak to the lock keeper and explained that we would let them go through together, on the understanding that we would then enter the lock when the next group exited towards us, we were hoping then we would perhaps have less boats in the lock. The area around the lock was extremely busy, there were two locks keepers working, one of them standing under a canopy to shield himself from the sun, surrounded by onlookers, all chatting, children were running around the top of the locks, evidently this was the place for a social gathering. There was also a display of metal sculptures for sale and a blacksmith type workshop situated back from the lock quay.

After quite a long period of time, it appeared that neither locks were in operation, so I walked back across the road to the lock. I could see a crowd gathered on the footbridge over the top of the lock, I wondered what they were looking at. Nothing, as both locks were empty. I enquired to the lock keeper, why the locks were empty, as there was about eight boats waiting on the other side to us, and he informed me that he was waiting for a hotel barge to arrive, and that everyone must wait. It was a very hot day and my temper was similar to the temperature, increasing rapidly. I commented that I understood that hotel barges took priority over other pleasure craft, but not when the boat was nowhere to be seen. He was filling two locks up so that the boat could enter, empty, it was ludicrous and a waste of water, the very thing that we are lectured about. Every few days we would receive leaflets stating that we must not waste water and share locks. Instead of sending one set of boats up and through the two locks, while he waited for the hotel barge to arrive, he had chosen to fill the locks without any boats in, thus creating a bottle neck of boats on either side of the locks waiting to enter. I stormed back to our boat, muttering that the lock keeper was a cretin and then explained to everyone waiting on our side, exactly what was occurring. Perhaps an hour later, we finally entered the lock, as I had to walk back with my long stick to lift the rope off the bow of the deck and for Jeff to pass up the stern rope, I needed a reasonable amount of space. The quay was still full of people, and *Fernando Alonso*, as I had named him, due to his resemblance to the Spanish Racing Driver, mirrored sunglasses and dark curly hair, seemed to be putting on a show for his spectators, dashing around on the quay. As obviously, he didn't need to take any ropes from us, he returned to his kiosk under the parasol and chatted to the passers-by, what he failed to do was to operate any level of health and safety. The hangers on, where blocking the access between one lock and the other so I couldn't walk a rope through, which I would normally do and with my extra-long pole, I could easily have knocked one of the small children, with legs dangling over the edge of the lock into the lock, but he was too busy, showing off, white teeth dazzling his fans, to take any notice of the safety of anyone.

When we finally left the second lock, instead of thanking him for opening the lock and giving him a smile, as I usually would, I glared at him, and got back on the boat in a huff. I hoped I wouldn't encounter any more *Alonso's* on the way. The problem with cruising in the summer holidays, is the staff working on the locks are often inexperienced summer temps. On one occasion, we were in a lock on the Champagne Bourgogne canal and two youngsters, a boy and a girl arrived in VNF uniform on scooters. They were not needed to operate the lock, they were obviously supposed to be maintaining the system. The girl proceeded to pull weeds from the edge of the lock, resulting in clumps of dirt, gravel and grass showering our lovely white boat. As you can imagine, I was not amused. Having had a teenager, I can fully appreciate the brain not indicating the consequences of their actions, but with temporary lock keepers, some are power crazy, like *Alonso, (he probably got picked on at school,)* some don't give a hoot, and some are simply clueless. It was obviously going to be one of those days.

Not much further along the canal was another set of double locks, as we approached it was evidently not as entertaining as the last set, as there wasn't anyone lingering. A lone girl stood in her uniform of light blue polo shirt and navy-blue shorts. We entered the lock without any problems, and tied the ropes. The girls was standing under her sunshade, in her own little world, nothing seemed to be happening, she had given me the thumbs up that she was going to activate the lock, then I noticed that one of the lock gates, which she had closed behind us, had swung open again.

Eventually, I managed to attract her attention, and she pressed her button on her 'PlayStation handset,' that she was carrying about and the gate closed again, and the lock started filling up.

When we exited, I thanked her and told her we were going to moor before the next lock and would start at nine the next morning. As all the locks are manual, each boat has to inform the lock keeper what time they want to set off so that the there is someone at the lock, otherwise you are stuck. In the summer, there are so many boats coming along, that once the first boat is booked then I suspect that the lock keeper stays put for the day but frustratingly, nine o clock, doesn't mean the lock with be open at nine, it means that they will arrive at nine, open the door to their station, have a cigarette and about nine fifteen wander out and press the button to start the lock filling up. You can't plan a day on the Midi, the lock keepers decide how long your day will take.

We tied up just above the lock, next to a boat that had obviously been abandoned, the wooden posts in the ground broken so, after our long and frustrating day, time to get the sledge hammer out again. Unfortunately, I had learnt the hard way that the post was broken, after putting a rope around it, and it coming-out of the ground with the rope attached. It seemed like a nice quiet spot, *Matilda* could go outside, and the plane trees remained untouched along the stretch, creating a shady walk to the next lock. Jeff, took *Bilbo* to check out the lock for any irregularities as the first locks of the morning would be a triple, at 8,73m high, so over three metres higher than the last lot, and five metres higher than some that we had done that day, so more of a challenge. After dinner, I took *Bilbo* for second walk, so I could look at the lock and see where the bollards are positioned, the Captain and crew seek different information, I need to look to see where I will put a rope, Jeff needs to decide where he will position the boat in the lock, depending on the shape of the lock walls and where the bollards are.

As we walked back, a group of people on a hire boat, said *Hello*, as is the norm, they wanted to know what breed *Bilbo* was. They were Welsh, and were most amused to discover that he was a Welsh Fox Hound. I chatted for a while, a nice friendly bunch, and parted, with the comment, we would see them in the lock in the morning. The sun broke through the trees, and it was soon time to set off. I took *Bilbo* for his morning walk, it was a glorious morning, and I was enjoying the tranquillity, as I was walking, I noticed a boating pole floating in the water, so crouched down and fished it out. It was a lightweight one, the type that hire boats use. As it is not unusual to lose poles, our friend Mick, lost his own, then Richards, who he was travelling in convoy with, I thought it would come in useful, somebody always needs a spare one. As we had lots of spare time until left, Jeff walked *Bilbo* up to the lock again and chatted to the Welsh people discussing tactics, the best place for them to be positioned next to us. At nine o clock, Jeff approached the lock and as I walked up, I spied the lock keeper getting out of his car, Oh No, it was *Alonso*, back to torture me for another day.

The three locks were a doddle for us, but the hire boaters were having a nightmare on the other side of the lock. Perhaps the attire of sarongs and flipflops were not the best choice for running around the deck of a boat. As we were tied up relatively quickly, *Alonso* not giving us a hard time, perhaps he had a good night's sleep, we were able to observe the antics on the hireboats. In the first lock, one of the chaps was standing on the lock wall, waiting for one of the ladies in their wafty outfits to throw a rope up. After several unsuccessful attempts, not surprising as the lock was so high, I called across to them to put the rope on a pole and pass it up. After much searching the couldn't find the boat hook and eventually the other man managed to throw the rope up, but it wasn't attached to the boat! It took quite a long time for the two ropes to be attached and the lock to be finally activated, then someone noticed that there were some ducks in the lock. One of the Welsh ladies started hollering at the man on the side of the lock, who then asked *Alonso* to open the lock again, so he opened the lock and we waited for the ducks to come out! By lock three, they had got into the swing of things and the last lock was not such a drama but as they exited the last lock, I heard one of them call to the other "Have you found that stick yet? "I think perhaps they had dropped theirs overboard, the previous day and I had found it, but they steamed off past us as they were on the way back to their hire base. Oh well, I am sure someone else I know will need a stick! In twenty-four hours we had acquired two fenders and a pole, and left a barbeque and two life rings at Capestang, maybe it was karma for the broken flag pole, an exchange system for boaters.

The three locks were a doddle for us, but the hire boaters were having a nightmare on the other side of the lock. Perhaps the attire of sarongs and flipflops were not the best choice for running around the deck of a boat. As we were tied up relatively quickly, Alonso not giving us a hard time, perhaps he had a good night's sleep, we were able to observe the antics on the hireboats. In the first lock, one of the chaps was standing on the lock wall, waiting for one of the ladies in their floaty outfits to throw a rope up. After several unsuccessful attempts, not surprising as the lock was so high, I called across to them to put the rope on a pole and pass it up. After much searching the couldn't find the stick and eventually the other man managed to throw the rope up, but it wasn't attached to the boat! It took quite a long time for the two ropes to be attached and the lock to be finally activated, then someone noticed that there were some ducks in the lock. One of the Welsh ladies started hollering at the man on the side of the lock, who then asked *Alonso* to open the lock again, so he opened the lock and we waited for the ducks to come out! By lock three, they had got into the swing of things and the last lock was not such a drama but as they exited the last lock, I heard one of them call to the other "Have you found that stick yet? "I think perhaps they had dropped theirs overboard, the previous day and I had found it, but they steamed off past us as they were on the way back to their hire base. Oh well, I am sure someone else I know will need a stick! In twenty-four hours we had acquired two fenders and a pole, and left a barbeque and two life rings at Capestang, maybe it was karma for the broken flag pole an exchange system for boaters.

We had hoped to stop at the small town of Marseillette, marked on the map as having an open air café, boulangerie and a small town centre but as we approached the narrow bridge the wind was strong and we were struggled to get through without dinging the sides, by the time we had negotiated through we were upon the mooring and not in any position to stop, having already missed one lot and disappointedly we couldn't turn round, the canal was far too busy for such antics with boats coming either way, but our length would have caused a struggle on a good day. We marked it on our map as a nice mooring, one day, when we make the journey back, perhaps we will stop then.

We carried slowly along the canal, and shortly after Marseillette, instead of finding golden fields in our view, we saw cliffs with small nests of European bee eaters. That's the wonderful thing about canal life, each corner brings a new treat. A few more corners and many trees later, we arrived at the entrance to another set of three locks, this time not with a mad lockkeeper, I think we had left his section, but lined with splendid water mills, overlooking the locks one of the, had been part converted into a restaurant, the wisteria covered terrace overlooking the lock with a barrier to keep the public at bay, constructed of wine casks placed, closely but intermittently. Also, I suspect, as a vague nod at health and safety, to prevent the children of diners at the restaurants, ending up in the locks. A number of boats were already lined up waiting to enter, so we tied up at the superb pre- lock mooring, sheltered under the trees, and took *Bilbo* for a stroll. By the time we had returned, the boats were coming down the lock towards us and it was our turn next.

We arrived to moor up along the bank in Trebes, obviously an early victim of the tree culling, the bank had new plantations of Platanor, which apparently is resistant to the nasty disease that the plane trees have been victim to. Oblivious to the fact that the trees were samplings, to my annoyance, there were hire boats tied up to them. We found a perfect spot, opposite an olive grove and far enough away from the area accessible by car for our *Matilda* to have some freedom and put our stakes in. Arriving just before lunch, I scooted up to the tourist office, situated conveniently along the quay opposite a hire boat base. As I entered, the rush of cool air hit me, somewhere with air conditioning. I think I need to ask lots of questions! The purpose of trip, was to locate the nearest bus stop and time table. I left armed with a map of the town. The tourist office, like many on the Canal du Midi, sold a plethora of products, most notably an excellent regional wine selection and a display of products made from the olives growing opposite our boat. I felt a shopping frenzy, in fact, a good excuse to keep returning to the air conditioning.

The bus was due to arrive at 6.15, a short walk from where we were moored through the town. It gave us the opportunity to see more of Trebes, not the prettiest of towns, the outskirts look quite run down, the narrow streets housing families, the children playing in the gutter, whilst their mothers smoked, holding another baby to the hip. The hidden sights from the tourists. The bus stop was situated on the main road out of the town with the river Aude running under it. Just behind the bus stop, on the river bank, an Italian family had stopped in the caravan, either ignorant of, or impervious, to the large sign stating no camping. I can understand why they had stopped, it was a lovely spot, if a little noisy, with the main road to Carcassonne situated above it, lorries crossing the bridge to negotiate the limited space.

As there were bus stops on either side of the road, we were not convinced as to which side the bus would stop, so we positioned ourselves on either side. We may as well not have bothered, as forty-five minutes later, the bus had not arrived. We returned to the boat, bemused. Our walk had allowed us a peek of the town, a tiny square with a bank, a shop selling Portuguese produce, closed for the summer. A Butchers and bakers and a newsagent. Further along, towards the bridge over the canal, was a small Epicierie, (Supermarket), this too was closed for a month. I can appreciate small businesses closing in the school holidays, but this is a tourist resort, with a huge fleet of hireboats, to not have one food shop open in July seemed insane to me.

The jewel in Trebes crown, is most certainly its harbour quay. A small selection of restaurants flag the quay, in the middle of which is a wine bar. All of them seemed to be doing a roaring trade, open from late morning for coffees, they served straight through, something that is only found in big resorts, I suspect that if you tried to eat in October, you would be lucky to get a pizza, as we have driven there previously, and the town looked closed up but for three months, the staff obviously worked there socks off.

The following morning, I was delighted to be able to walk to the boulangerie and buy fresh croissants and bread, we were not cruising for a few days as we had done five days on the trot in searing heat and we were way ahead of schedule. We needed to be moored somewhere we could leave the boat for the end of August as our daughter was coming out for a week's holiday, then we were going back with her to help her move into halls at University. The restaurant staff were already washing the pavements in between their terraces and the entrances, separated by a road. After a return to the tourist office and some purchases of local wines to take home, and a few to try naturally. I explained to the staff that the bus had failed to arrive. I wondered whether it was a special service. The village we had lived in for three years, had a bus service that only ran during term time, if you wanted to get into town in July and August, you would be walking. The receptionist explained that it was necessary to telephone and book the bus, it would have been helpful if someone had told us that the day before. We had made two journeys to the bus stop the previous day, one with Bilbo, a walk to find the bus stop and work out how long it would take to get there, the second, later in the day, to catch the actual bus. I returned to the boat and rang the company, as was told that we had to make the reservation the day before, so I booked for the following evening, we definitely weren't going anywhere for a while!

Later that afternoon, we had a tap on the window, and heard an English voice. It belonged to the owner of one of the boats that had been locked up when we had arrived, he and his partner had just returned from a visit to the Uk and when he walked passed our boat had noticed the English flag, and wondered if we had any satellite reception as we had our dish up. We explained we were picking up about four channels. After a chat we bade farewell. Lynne and Steve, the boat owners, had the most adorable dog, a Parson's Terrier, the same breed as our friend Micks 'Billy. *Bilbo* and *Billy* had been great friends and *Bilbo,* as ever was enthusiastic to make a friend. In between the scorching heat and an occasional rain cloud, the two dogs became friends, as did their owners. As we were on a mission to retrieve the car from Homps, we arranged to have tapas at the wine bar on the quay one evening, and Lynne and Steve came onboard for drinks another. Embarrassingly, because Jeff had broken the table several weeks earlier, we had a hotpotch of tables on the deck with our new rug, which I wasn't convinced went with the colour of the deck paint. When we had bought the boat, it came with a carpet, I abhor carpet on decks, our first boat had one, and they always end up a soggy, smelly mess. When we took up the carpet the deck was not in a good state and Jeff had painted it with a grey deck paint, which we had used on our last boat *Maranatha*, I didn't like it, but the rug was supposed to go with the grey paint, generally it all looked a bit of a mish mash but as we were heading the same direction, I promised I would cook dinner at a later date, as we evidently needed to buy a new table. Jeff, who is normally very good at things like that admitted defeat, the aluminium had bent, and the table needed to go to the dustbins!

Towards the end of the week, was an evening market, something the Canal du Midi is famous for. The schedule for July and August, stopping in the larger towns, along the banks of the Midi, artisans travel selling their wares. Steve and Lynda invited us on for drinks, we left *Bilbo* on guard duty, his bark so loud, if someone came near the boat we would hear that before our burglar alarm, and Rollo, was on their deck, running up and down barking at anyone that dared to come near their boat. Lynda and I had planned to have a look around the market, but as we saw the stall holders setting up, established it was 'a load of old toot' and decided to stay onboard. The stalls packed up, but people milled around along the canal bank until the wee hours, the ambient temperatures, encouraging them to stay outdoors. This was not so good for Matilda, as we had locked her in the boat, early evening, we had taken to letting her out around midnight, as the last of the dog walkers would normally be gone but in this instance, they were still ambling about at two in the morning. She had to wait until the morning, when we could let her out and she would return to her new favourite place, in the middle of the olive groves.

The olive growers, *The Domaine des Peres*, had a large shop attached to its premises, with a sign with opening hours. I would not fulfil my tourist quota as I failed to enter the premises, despite several attempts. After the third time, when it still wasn't open, I bought various products from the tourist shop again, some to take home for my parents and some to keep, including the most fabulous lemon flavoured olive oil, which is great on prawns, well on anything really. There is nothing better than using something that you have seen growing from your window, unless I suppose it is growing them yourself, but after an unsuccessful attempt at a vegetable patch in our last house, which already had an abundance of cranberries and rhubarb, I failed to grow anything, so I am not green fingered. It was lucky that further along the same track as the olive growers, was another shop selling locally grown produce, so at least I could buy things with earth on them and fantasise they were mine.

After various dog walks along the canal, one hot Sunday, we decided to take the dogs to the lake. *Bilbo* is nervous in traffic and I was holding him tightly to me, but once we arrived at the lake I let him off with *Rollo*. *Bilbo* was his usual embarrassing self, instead of swimming in the lake with *Rollo*, he teetered around the edge, meanwhile *Rollo* was taking full benefit of the cooling water. When two men arrived under the guise of fishing, but evidently to have an afternoon away from home, drinking beer, they let their dog out of the car. A female Boxer dog, one of *Bilbo's* favourites breeds, as a girl boxer taught him to box, when he was a puppy, he instantly lost interest in poor *Rollo* and dashed around after her, but when she went into the water, he stood in the margins, what a wuss my dog is. It would be another two summers before I finally saw *Bilbo* swim properly when we were in Holland, and then he wouldn't come back, so perhaps I was best leaving him be, however a dog on a boat not being able to swim, particular one as big and heavy as *Bilbo*, is not the greatest thing in the world, but at least he isn't jumping over the side of the boat. We returned back to our respective boats, *Bilbo* as hot as before he left as all he had done was tear about.

Before we left Trebes, we did what lots of boaters do, swap DVD's, and a most odd thing occurred. When we had been moored in St Jean de Losne, we were having drinks with Robyn and Mike and she told me about a book that I should read called "Follow the Rabbit Proof Fence", I had made a note of it, as I often do when recommended but this stuck in my mind. The book, tells the story of mixed race children being taken away from their families to a training camp, to prevent further mixed-race children by teaching them to be "White "and keeping them away from fellow Aboriginals, the fence being constructed to keep them in. The idea being to eventually extinguish the race. I admit like many Brits of my age group, I am fairly ignorant to Australian history and when I was told that this was based on reality, I was pretty shocked.

In amongst the collection of DVDs that we had swapped, to my surprise and delight was "Rabbit Proof Fence ", starring Kenneth Brannagh. How strange that three months before I hadn't ever heard of the book and now I had a copy of the DVD, and I wonder, would I have watched it, if Robyn hadn't pre empted me to, or would I have thought it wasn't my thing and put it on the next pile to swap? Boating isn't all messing around on the water, particularly in Europe, it opens your eyes to new cultures, as they say, every day is a school day!

Leaving Trebes the natural next mooring would be Carcassonne, however, we intended on passing straight through. We had visited Carcassonne one winter, when visiting our friends in Castelnaudary. As it was early December, an ice rink was erected in the square and we had drunk coffee and hot chocolate, wrapped up woolly mufflers, observing the skaters joyously zipping pass. Even in December, with the all the shops closed, all the tables in the cafes were occupied. The café culture of sunglasses and thick jackets, with 112 days of sunshine per year, going out without your sunglasses is surely foolish! We had gone to Carcassonne on a dual mission, to see the landscape that inspired Kate Mosse to write her *Labyrinth* series and Walt Disney's fairy tale castle and to consider the port for future mooring. Regrettably, finding a parking space near the port, we drove behind the train station, in close vicinity. A number of vagrants had set up home, evidently, this is not uncommon. Although, it seems like a pleasant mooring, the sun on one side of the port, where the permanent winter berths lay, seemed to have left until Spring, not ideal if you plan to stay onboard, which was our intention. On the opposite side of the port, we strolled along enjoying the coolness in the air, the sun warming our noses, however, I felt edgy, that any minute we were about to be mugged, the tourists gone from the canal, only the undesirables remaining. We concluded that we definitely didn't want to moor in

Carcassonne, but if we were moored on the Midi, we wouldn't ever be far away from the turrets and ancient walls that were the real draw. The jewel in Carcassonne's crown is not seen easily from the canal, but as we did pass through on our boat, the port was buzzing, hotel barges lined up along the banks and hire boats filling the port. We passed by, relived not to be in the centre of the mayhem, passing high stone walls and narrow entrances we escaped into the countryside and to pass the plush green fields and towering sunflowers to make our way to Castelnaudary.

Chapter Nine

Old Friends and New

The bridge from into the port of Castelnaudary

After what seemed like an eternity, we arrived at the outskirts of Castelnaudary. It had been another long hot Sunday. After a stop at lunch time, *Bilbo* and I walked onto the next locks and returned to confirm that perhaps it was better to try and stop before the town. On the way, I managed to find some English people that lived in the town, walking along the towpath. *Bilbo's* desire to interact with every person and animal along the way, generally resulting in contact. The locks had attracted the usual collection of afternoon strollers and dog walkers, oblivious to the danger of peering over the edge when people are throwing ropes and poles about. As one of the Canal de Midi's highlights, the four locks of St Roch, it was understandable, why watch one boat go through a lock, when you can watch several go through four! As we attempted to moor the water was fairly shallow along the bank and it took several attempts to find a suitable depth to tie up safely, the proceedings being observed by the spectators at the lock. Once we had tied up, we took *Bilbo* over to the locks, so we could look to see where we would position ourselves. The lock keeper was sitting in a tower above the locks away from the annoying passers-by. I climbed the steep stone stairs of the tower and knocked on his door, arranging to go through the lock the following morning.

We were moored on the opposite side to the four locks, giving the opportunity for *Matilda* to interact on the path with the local geese. The path was quite busy, I had already walked backwards into some cyclists as I pulled the ropes to the pull the boat in, and we soon discovered that despite the tow path leading to nowhere, it was used as a cut through, so poor *Matilda* had to get back on the boat, as I she had taken to freezing in the middle of the path rather than moving to one side. *Bilbo* was terrified of the geese, who flocked to the end of our bow, honking repeatedly at him.

After dinner, we walked into Castelnaudary towards the port, and found our friends sitting at a table in the local wine cave, waiting for a wine tasting lecture, when their two dogs saw *Bilbo*, there was much barking, and we retired for the evening, leaving them to their wine before we caused too much disturbance.

Despite having stayed in Castelnaudary countless times, we haven't ever been there when the canal was open, and boats going through. With this in mind, when we exited the locks to enter an island before the port called the Grand Basin, we were unsure of which way to go. We went the wrong side, and approached a bridge before the port at a funny angle, scraping the roof of the boat, and making an early morning entrance! The port itself was full, but we moored further along the bank, with lots of other boats. Now this area is being made into further moorings with facilities, but we were lucky enough to moor for free at the time. Within minutes of tying up, our friends Sally and Glenn arrived with their two dogs, *Haggis* and *Deliah*. *Deliah* was a recent addition, we had met her, and walked her the previous winter, but *Bilbo* hadn't as he was at the dog B and B and we were on our way to Spain. He was and delighted to see his friend *Haggis*, a black cockerpoo, who he had spent many hours playing with, but he was a bit perturbed that Deliah kept barking at him. Although our friends had seen us each winter, the last time we were on a boat, it was our last one, and *Haggis* used to come aboard for biscuits, now we had *Matilda* aboard, so I stupidly shut her in the bedroom whilst they had a look and she promptly peed on the bed! Not an ideal start.

We had arrived on a Monday, which, in Castelnaudary is market day. Glenn, Sally, their dogs and I walked into town and around the massive market chatting. *Bilbo* is not good with crowded places and I left him on the boat, with Jeff, how we got around a market with lots of food and two dogs I don't know, but they were remarkably well behaved. It also happened to be Jeff's Sixty Fifth birthday, we had hoped to arrive in time to celebrate with our friends but as with all boating trips, you are never certain you will be where you are supposed to. After inviting them for drinks that evening, when I mentioned it was Jeff's birthday, Sally promptly asked the local bar owner if he would open that evening as he normally took the night off. By lunchtime, Sally had organised a gathering that evening with the boat locals.

Back to the boat and it was time for me to do some organising of our own. Our solar charge controller had stopped working and when we left Trebes we were armed with a mobile number of an engineer within the region, and as we intended on staying in Castelnaudary for some time, it seems like the ideal time to call for assistance. With an appointment organised for the following day, we could get on with settling into our new surroundings. We were moored opposite the fire station and we had our own theatre taking place, with the daily preparations by the pompiers. Adjacent to the fire station, was a sports hall and on the grounds outside, a selection of mature gentleman played petanque. The banks of the canal filled with picnickers sheltering under the plane trees, and in the afternoon a passenger boat speeded past, causing the boat to rock and roll. Life was happening all around, a new back drop, new routines to observe. Sally and I took the dogs for a walk and by the time we had returned our friendly dogs had charmed an old man, shame our French couldn't do the same, but for the rest of the time we were in Castelnaudary, every day I would see him out walking and we would stop and chat.

When we arrived at the bar that evening, two tables long tables were full of people Sally had invited out for a drink. Jeff doesn't like a lot of fuss but appreciated the birthday cake that Sally had purchased and a chorus of "Happy Birthday". The evening was spent with a delightful collection of people, much wine was drunk and common interests found. Having spent many hours over the years in the local wine bar, situated on the quay, it was lovely to be there in the summer, watching the sun go down and enjoying the coolness of the night, instead of being inside with jumpers on and the heating. With the arrival of Haggis and Deliah, it was soon time to take our own mutt for a stroll along the banks, and let *Matilda* out, under supervision. The walk having the effect of sobering me up, sufficiently to not feel as awful as I should have the following morning, which was fortunate, as the engineer came to look at our solar charge controller at Nine am, when I may have taken the opportunity to go back to bed after walking *Bilbo*, in other circumstances.

After purchasing a digital multi control from him, which hadn't worked since the first day we cruised in Holland, with Jeff and Bruce, enthusiastically trying everything out, the guy took our charge controller away to repair it. Although we had already replaced it ourselves, the Victron, which was not working, cost seven hundred pounds, so not something to throw away. We had bought them over the years for the lake building, and a spare is always handy. He left with our controller and we didn't ever see him again! He didn't answer his phone, I texted and emailed, to no response, we had been duped!

Castelnaudary is famous for two things, Cassoulet and the Foreign Legion. Cassoulet, I cannot abide, and we have dined out in the town on our previous visits and unless you want to eat Cassoulet, there is little choice. The famous French Foreign Legion, based in the town since 1975, held considerable more interest. Once a week a bus arrived in town and the men poured out in their smart uniforms to sit in the cafes and walk through the town. During the week, with my canal side view, I would be lucky enough to watch them running along the towpath. If you like a man in uniform, Castelnaudary is definitely the place to be!

A few days after we arrived, we headed off to Toulouse in search of new table for our deck, but returned empty handed but on a trip to one of the out of town stores in Castelnaudary, whilst searching for something for my mother, I came upon a hardwood table. I returned with a table, and a rug for the deck. We were now back to having an outside entertaining space, which coincided with the arrival of Steve, Lynda and *Rollo*, conveniently arriving in time to attend a Polynesian Festival. They enthusiastically walked up to see what was occurring, we could hear the music, and had done since nine that morning when they started setting up, they returned an hour later. As with many of these events, you really need to be French to appreciate them, or in a big group. When I walked *Bilbo* the following morning, some of the people were sitting around in a circle singing, they were obviously having a great time.

Sunday evening was Wine Tasting night, as opposed to wine drinking night, which seemed to be every night in Castelnaudary! We had missed it the previous week, but it was the perfect opportunity for Steve and Lynda to meet the rest of the group, had we actually had any wine before ten that evening. The premise was that we tried various wines whilst a French lady told us all about them, and we had appropriate food, i.e. goats cheese with the white and mini gateaux with the desert wine. It was a long evening and when it finished we were all keen to buy some of the wine we had sampled, but in the usual half-cocked French way, she had demonstrated wine that was not in stock in the bar, serious lack of communication there. We compromised, chose something available, and tried to make the most of the evening, happy to be outside, after spending the evening sitting inside the stuffy bar. Perhaps the lack of air was contributory, or too many wines mixed, as we were swallowing, not spitting, but as we returned to our boat, instead of scrambling down the bank, something I had become adept to, I promptly fell down it. Some nasty bruising resulted, and an admission that wearing wedges, when you have to mountaineer to get back to your boat, was not advisable.

Tuesday evening, we were invited to dinner onboard *Louisa* a stunning hotel barge, owned by an English couple. There were ten of us in total, and a fabulous meal was had by all, and after dinner, we all danced on the extremely large deck. I was starting to feel as though as I was on holiday, every day something was happening, the joys of endless hot nights. On Thursday evening, was a night market on the quay, a considerable improvement on the one at Trebes, but as we were moored away from the main port, I wandered on my own, leaving Jeff onboard as security.

Friday evening, there was a Jazz concert in the square. Having been to many of these events when we lived in Vitry, we didn't have high expectations, but Lynda and Steve were prepared with a picnic, there was light drizzle, and Lynda and I had do buy some dodgy house wine in plastic cups, to avail ourselves of the toilet facilities in the local bar. Unlike Vitry, the bars did not have tables set up outside encouraging us to enjoy the music with a carafe of wine, instead, plastic vending machine cups to take away and sit on a wall, not very dignified. The music was good, as was the company, had we gone on our own, we would have been bored to tears. This time, I walked the long way around to get to the boat, reducing the damage to myself as I was still feeling a little fragile from Sunday evening.

We had made the decision to stay in Castelnaudary until our daughter visited and leave the boat in port, whilst we returned to the Uk with her to move her into halls at University. With this in mind, we decided to get some tiling done in our shower. Initially we had visited the local Brico shops to try and find something suitable other than tiles, but gave up and called a tiler. As we had previous experience of French workmanship, our expectations were not too high, but it was a small job. Had we still had our lakes we had a tile cutter and other equipment, so we could have done it ourselves, but buying more equipment for the job seemed silly, better to get a professional.

The chap came was accompanied by his son, he looked at the job and arranged to come back the following week. It was fortunate, that he had brought his son, his apprentice with him, as the son spoke reasonable English as *Lisa the Linguistics* vocabulary does not include, grout! The day that they came to do the job, was perhaps not the best choice. It was the first day of the annual Cassoulet Festival, a three-day event, to celebrate Cassoulet. It is one of the things we love about France, I am sure if there was a Festival of Lancashire Hot Pot it would not be greeted with the same enthusiasm.

The port had been evacuated, as on Saturday, there was to be a water festival taking place, our friends boats had all moved further away from the town into the grand basin. We, luckily, were able to stay in position, with boats joining us along the bank. When the men arrived to do the tiling, they couldn't park anywhere near us as the streets were blocked off, additional parking had been made on the site where the Polynesian festival had taken place and they had to drop their tools off then park the van. Not a good start. Whilst people were walking along the bank, the man was cutting tiles outside our boat, and Jeff and I sat with our two pets, *Matilda*, on a lead attached to my chair and *Bilbo* attached to Jeff's, as the doors needed to be kept open for the men to come in and out. I think they had chosen the busiest and hottest day of the year and the father wasn't exactly slim, squeezing himself into our shower room, on his bulging stomach to get access to the floor.

Job done, they left, grateful to get away from the noise and the heat. leaving me to clean up, something I have found common with French workmen, they don't ever clear up after themselves, on a plus point, instead of the cracked tiles on the floor which were on the boat when we bought her with had nice new grey ones, updating the bathroom. With the recent additions to the deck, new fenders and paint, our boat was looking top notch, time to have a rest.

The Festival of Cassoulet, brought hoards to the town, walking day and night along the canal. Effectively, it was lots of stalls selling Cassoulet with an excuse for a party. Live Music was playing at various times of the   and the sound of voices on the loud speaker echoed. On Saturday, we attended the beginning of the water sports antics, which were a collection of handmade boats of various shapes and sizes in a race, sponsored by local companies. It was amusing as none of them looked water worthy, they were like the kind of contraptions that you would expect Jeremy Clarkson and James May to be racing against each other in, with perhaps less finesse.

Saturday evening, we chose not to stand with the hoards and watch the live music, we could hear it from the deck of our boat, but we decided to take a picnic onto the bank outside our boat, stupidly, I had forgotten the ants that had bitten me voraciously when we were putting the new fenders onto the boat the previous week, quickly our food was overrun with ants. We retreated to the safety of our deck, the local ducks benefitting from my error. I spent the rest of the evening scratching, convinced that they were running all over me.

The last stragglers left around three the following morning, and we finally got to sleep, only to be woken by the fire engines being cleaned at around eight. Keen to avoid the crowds, I took *Bilbo* for a walk and noticed that someone had put a chair on the bow of our boat! There were various points throughout the town, with fold up chairs and someone had obviously decided to leave theirs on our boat, rather than return it to the point. I hastily grabbed it and carried it to the nearest point, lest someone think we had stolen it. What I find amazing is that in order to put the chair on the boat, you would need to climb on, and neither us, or *Bilbo* had woken up.

Sunday there were processions, and more music, and by late afternoon the crowds started to disperse. By Monday lunchtime, it was all cleared away, as though it had never existed. As the bar had been busy all weekend, there wasn't any wine tasting, and the port looked strangely empty, until everyone dashed back to get their places.

Jousting at Castelnaudary

When we arrived in Castelnaudary, Sally had told me that the leisure centre, opposite where we were moored, housed an outdoor swimming pool. Since we had arrived intended on going for a swim, but I had given up trying to go with someone else and decided to go alone. I waited until the hottest part of the day, suspecting the cool waters would be all the more refreshing, but I found the heat overhead intolerable, and remained in the quieter indoor pool. As I was swimming, there was a young boy in the pool on his own, his mother sitting on a bench, when he exited the pool, she followed him back through to the changing rooms, which meant you had to walk through a foot bath. As she was dressed head to toe in a hijab, which got soaked. I found this poignant, that in order to supervise her son, she had subjected herself wetting all her clothes, she could have lifted them up, but she walked through with clothes to the floor and her shoes on, it was very bizarre, I am sure she really wanted to dip in the chilled water. I had not enjoyed my swimming experience, perhaps the recommendations were made having swum off season, but the majority of the people in both pools were teenage boys, I wouldn't have a hope of getting our daughter in the pool on her visit, which was a shame as we both love swimming, but she had received enough harassment over the years living in France, that knowing what it was like, I wouldn't suggest it.

One hot day, on recommendation, we took *Bilbo* over to one of the nearby lakes. Unfortunately, there were two in the region, and *he that is always right*, insisted that we went to one, when I was sure we were supposed to go to the other one. After driving round, trying to find an entrance, we eventually stopped when we saw a dog swimming in the water. As it seemed safe, once we were far enough from the road, I let *Bilbo* off his lead. He can move at lot quicker than us, and dashed off towards the water, to be met with hysterical shrieks. A large lady was swimming in the water and when she saw *Bilbo* started shouting, the problem was not our dog, but hers, which was also in the water. The other problem was that she didn't have any clothes on, ours not hers, as she dashed out of the water and ran towards her dog. Meanwhile *Bilbo* advanced towards her dog, tail wagging. The two dogs met, and dashed about together in a friendly fashion, but we had obviously disturbed her peace and privacy, and when we could catch him, we retrieved *Bilbo* apologising and made a sharp exit. On the plus side, we had seen a new part of the area, and field after field of sunflowers, which one can't ever complain about, unless you were a sunflower picker!

Later that week, Sally had organised a trip to a vineyard for all of us. Jeff volunteered to drive one group, and we set off in search of a village tucked away in the hills. It was a Deja vous of when we first arrived in France and my mother, daughter and I were taken for a champagne tasting, but at least this time, I trusted the driver implicitly. I did feel like we were going on a school trip as we tried to find the village, and were grateful when we found David's car with the rest of the group. Sadly, after a week of fabulous weather, the afternoon was drizzly, and we were all a little cold, in our summer clothes, but not to be deterred we followed our hostess through the vineyard, where she cut grapes off for us to try and demonstrated how they were cut. It was fascinating, and we were treated to fabulous views of the region from a superb vantage point. Returning to the store where the wine was pressed, we were then given a laid-back wine tasting, culminating in the inevitable purchasing of said products. We were all familiar with her wines as they were stocked in the local wine bar but it's not the same as buying direct from the manufacturer. Jeff, as driver abstained, so Sally got the benefit of tasting all his wine samples, a reward for being the organiser, and once again adding to the holiday feel.

As you probably gathered, we had done little sightseeing, in Castelnaudary, the blazing sun from late morning until five in the afternoon, was hardly an encouragement, we tended to hide away during the day, appearing for a stroll with *Bilbo*. The castle of the towns name, had long since been destroyed by the Cathars. Later that week, Lynda, Steve and I went to an art exhibition in the old jail, originally attached to the Presidial, which was a Criminal and Civil Court, the jail was run until 1926. It is now a primary school, with an exhibition attached to the Musee Lauragais. It was remarkable to observe the buildings, what was also intriguing was why we were the only people inside. It felt rather odd wandering around, just the three of us, but Jeff and I had a similar experience year previously in Joinville in some beautiful gardens, there rarely seems to be anyone at these exhibits, unless you are in Paris, and then the queues are insanely long, as you would expect.

That evening, we arranged to meet Lynda and Steve for a drink in the wine cave. Sally and Glenn were preoccupied with guests with dogs and children onboard, and one of the boating couples were getting married at the weekend, so everyone was caught up in their plans. Our daughter was due to arrive in a few days, as was Lynda's son, so it was probably the last opportunity to get together before we split up to our new horizons.

I had recently bought a summer dress and decided to remind Jeff why he married me, and dress up a little, so I was wearing my dress and strappy heels, determined to not ski down the bank later, when we tried to get back on the boat. We arrived at the wine cave around eight and chose a bottle of wine, then Steve arrived and said Lynda was running late as she had just got out of the shower. At eight thirty, when Lynda had not arrived, Steve bought a bottle of Rose, as we had bought red and shortly afterwards Lynda arrived. Within fifteen minutes, Alan, the owner, told he was shutting up for the night, and could we drink up and go. Astonished, we asked him if we bought some more wine, could we stay and sit outside, none of us wanted to go back to our boats, so he agreed. Bizarrely, everyone else left and he told us to put the wine glasses under the shutter, and the bottles in the bottle bank! What a strange evening, we hadn't gone for the superb wine, we could have bought three bottles for the price of one, but for the enjoyment of going out in a nice environment. How strange people are.

With the arrival of one of the boats, came our post, a regular occurrence between certain ports for the expats, our post was important, we had new insurance documents, we had registered our car and caravan at Moissac, as this was to be our home port. Luckily, we did not need to change the number plate for the car, something which is a requirement of French cars over a certain age, but the caravan fell into latter category, therefore we needed to buy a new number plate before we towed the caravan next month. The last time I had bought a new number plate was in Vitry le Francois, where we used to live, we had moved to a new house and reregistered the car at the new address, resulting in a new number plate, what a mad system. The young guy who ordered it on my behalf, who I called "The Ginger One", made an error, and when I arrived he unwrapped the wrong number plate! I hoped that they would be more efficient in the South. So far, I had found that the main dealer for Seat, in Beziers charged less for a standard service than in Vitry, so perhaps things would be an improvement here.

Instead of being asked to return in a few days, I was asked to come back in an hour, just enough to time to hit the summer sales. We were going away in the winter to Spain, so I definitely needed to some shop summer, although I found myself looking wistfully at the autumn clothes that I had no need of. It would be the first winter I would not be working, or meeting my friend twice weekly for a coffee in Chez Maximes wrapped up in my winter clothes, no appointments at the bank, or lunches when friends visited, no house. I hadn't really considered it for a while, as we had been busy enjoying our boating, but I had a little twinge of regret for our old life. The season was nearly over, and usually I would be getting ready for the last two months at the lake, looking forward to seeing our clients return with their tales and ours of our adventures.

By later that week, the children went back to school. The morning air had a chill to it, summer was over. Early autumn had arrived, it was still warm during the day but the colourful hydrangeas in the gardens on the walk to school were just beginning to turn brown. I felt melancholy, as usually at this time of the year, we would be in a flurry of activity, with The Daughters imminent return to school, the last few weeks, spent visiting bookshops and stationers to purchase the necessary equipment. This year, she had done it all herself in England, and I had been excluded. When I saw the children walking to school, it seemed like a lifetime ago, since our daughter attended primary school in France, terrified that she couldn't speak any French, now she had passed her Brevet, her Baccalaureate, and studied at French university and was about to make her first step without us, to start University in England. Only a year ago, we had been carrying boxes up flights of stairs to her new apartment, only to carry them down again the following May when she moved out. She had achieved so much, and I still couldn't speak proper French!

When our daughter arrived, the weather had decided to be horrible, the first couple of days were cold and drizzly. Added to that, the usual problem when you have guests on board a boat, something breaks. This time it was our generator. By a stroke of luck, we were moored below a garage, so on our daughter's second day of her holiday, she got to put her French into practice, and accompany me to the garage and persuade a mechanic to come to our aid. It took him a short time to fix the problem, sometimes, it is better to ask a professional than to mess about with things you don't know about. It would have taken Jeff all day.

The Daughter and I had planned a trip to Carcassonne, leaving Jeff in charge of the pets. A girly day out was just what we needed. Arriving at the station.as we walked across the crossing into town, we approached at the traffic lights by a beggar. Not a good start, The Daughter has had a phobia about beggars, when she was about six, we caught the train to Norwich, and I gave someone begging with his dog, some money. She got on her moral high horse and told me she was going to "Tell Dad", knowing that he would not approve. It wasn't a lack of compassion, but an innate fear of beggars. As we started making frequent trips to France on the Eurostar, not once did we manage a journey without being approached by someone. In Italy, it was the lady begging outside Vatican City, admittedly she did look like the evil queen from *Sleeping Beauty*. When she moved to Nancy, the array of people lined along her daily walk, did not concern her, they were part of the daily wallpaper, but within minutes of arriving in Carcassonne, being harassed, reinforced my opinion of Carcassonne, and The Daughters of France in general. The previous evening, when we were out walking *Bilbo*, two young men, smoking a shisha pipe at one of the picnic tables made a comment, which obviously she understood, and thank fully, I did not. This was not helping my cause, to persuade her to return to France, permanently.

After a little shopping, we arrived at the beginning of the walk to the castle. You would have to be made of stone yourself, to not appreciate its splendour, but I wish we had got a bus! By the time, we walked there, we were both shattered. The grounds were knee deep in people and we decided to walk around the outskirts and wait until lunch time, when hopefully they would disperse. Sadly, the tourists obviously weren't French, as the crowds did not thin out, and we decided to abandon a full tour, and spend the entrance fee in one of the gift shops instead. A satisfactory solution! After that we returned to the main square and had lunch then visited some more shops, and got back on the train. I think she was keener to get back to her cat then look at some old buildings, even the alleged Disney fairy-tale castle didn't captivate her heart, she would soon be living in one of the most historic towns in England, stuffed full of wonderous architecture.

The week passed quickly, and it was soon time to make our way back to England. Our journey would take two days by car, stopping at Froncles for the night in France, we were dropping the pets off in Beziers, at the dog B and B with John and Ian. *Bilbo* was delighted, as ever to arrive there, *Matilda* wasn't quite so keen, it was her first time, as previously she had remained at home, with The Daughter, but they promised to let her out, when the other dogs were in the house, and with *Bilbo*. We had ordered some more fenders from the chandlers at St Jean de Losne so had arranged to see our friends Robyn and Mike for a cup of tea before we continued to Froncles. As our daughter was insured to drive the car, and hadn't driven since the previous summer, she was keen to drive, and took over for some of the journey, which was nail biting to say the least!

When we arrived in St Jean, we parked up and were alarmed to find that the chandlers was locked up. There had been building work taking place all year, for a new shop, and it seemed that the stock had been moved into the new shop, but only the cleaning lady was there. Annoyingly, our fenders were stacked up, with a note on the side with our name on them. After banging on the door and not getting any sense from the cleaner, except that Vasilly, the manager was not there, we decided to try an alternative. Nicholas, one of the sales team, who had dealt with the sale of our last boat *Maranatha*, was working, and he opened the shop up for us and got our fenders. We certainly didn't want to have to call in on the way back as we were collecting our new caravan from Froncles when we returned not an easy thing to negotiate narrow streets with.

When we arrived at Robyn and Mike's boat, she had made my favourite muffins. Their little dog *Harry*, had gone to London, to quarantine as they were flying back to New Zealand, in the next couple of weeks. As we chatted, I was filled with sadness, this would be the last time we saw them, more friends we had made that would never come back. As we said goodbye, I shed a tear, when our friends Bruce and Karen had gone back to New Zealand, I felt in my heart we would see them again someday, but with Robyn and Mike, it seemed final.

I didn't have much time to wallow, as soon we were in Froncles and I had new challenges to attend to. Having not slept in a caravan for at least fifteen years, after a day's travelling, I was not looking forward to the evening. When we arrived we first had to remove the cover protecting it from the harsh sun, then the contents, strewn hastily when the daughter moved from her apartment. My main concern, had been that the caravan had not become an ant farm as when we were transporting everything the car had filled with ants when parked next to the canal. Jeff wanted to put the new number plate on but couldn't find any tools in the chaos of the car. By the time we had finished this it was dark. This shouldn't have been a problem, had we managed to switch the electricity on! For some reason, we tried to plug the power cable into the wrong socket, as we had had the caravan plugged in, back in February when we bought it, you would have thought we would remember it, but it had been a long day. I quickly cooked some pasta on the hob, at least we had got the gas working, one night in the single beds was enough to realise that the caravan was not for us. We had purchased the caravan under the assumption that it had hot water. The hapless sales assistant had searched for the button to heat the water when we collected the caravan and had the engineers crawling all other to look for the hot water system. After paying for it, there was little we could do but take it away. We had thought perhaps we could get around it, but the beds topped it, it would have to go, something to address when we got back from the UK.

With more pressing matters to deal with, we needed to get back to England, and load the contents of my parent's garage into our car. The following day our daughter was collecting the keys for halls. Oxford here we come.

Chapter Ten

New Beginnings, New Adventures

A year on, we were moving our daughter again. Boxes full and car packed we arrived with the first load for her room. As we hadn't been present for the walk round it was all new to us. A French couple were looking for their daughters building, and our daughter chatted to them in French, I think they were relieved to have someone to converse with, if a little bewildered. It took me back to the previous year, when The Daughter and I were searching for apartments and her prospective landlady thought we were Swiss as my accent was definitely not French! After a look round, we returned to my parents' house, to load up with the rest of her belongings to return the following day. The single bed was a far cry from her lovely apartment in Nancy, but this was a new start, with lots of new people to meet. When we finally left her in her room unpacking, some of the other girls she was sharing with had already arrived, through the wonders of social media, they had already connected up, a far cry from the University in Nancy, where people attended places near to their home towns, with people they had known since primary school. Unlike University in France, we were not only an hour away, with regular trips home, we were in another country and when we left, knowing we would not see her again until Christmas, the distance seemed further away, despite the fact that most students don't go home until then anyway.

We left my parents with an empty nest, they had gone from relative peace to their granddaughter taking over their lives for four months, they left for holiday the following week and returned to a quiet house, I am sure they breathed a huge sigh of relief! Meanwhile, we returned to France and collected our caravan from Froncles, a second night did not improve our opinion. We had arranged to take the caravan into storage near to Castelnaudary, but parked up for the night near to the boat, upsetting a few motorhomers, as caravans are not popular in France, they think you are a gypsy! The following morning, we took the caravan to a beautiful house in a village with lustrous Rhododendron bushes ending the drive, not ideal when approaching in a caravan. We left it in storage in a barn next to the house, a little area for an office set up in the corner. It was only when we went to back it in that we realised that the lights were not working properly! When we had a new tow, bar fitted at the local garage they had evidently wired up the electrics wrong, and the lights were indicating opposite, we had travelled through France with the indicators given the wrong way, thank goodness, the gendarmes hadn't seen us.

After collecting *Bilbo* and *Matilda,* we returned to the boat to start preparations for leaving. The last leg of our journey this year onto the Tarn and Garonne. Within a week the atmosphere in the port had changed, *Louisa*, the hotel barge had left for Carcassonne, as it had clients arriving, Lynda and Steve had also gone to Carcassonne, cruising with some family, collecting others there and Sally and Glenn were waiting to take a slow trip to Toulouse to get some work done on their boat. After stocking up with supplies we drove to Moissac, our ultimate destination for the year and left the car there, catching the train back. It was a glorious day, and the port looked very inviting, I couldn't wait to get there. A train journey from Moissac to Toulouse then a wait at Toulouse gave us the chance for a quick look round, the outside of the train station was impressive, we would get to see the city by water in the next few weeks.

The second part of the train journey to Castelnaudary, was thankfully speedy as within five minutes of the train departing, it appeared we were in the same carriage as *The Train Nutter*. I do tend to attract them, for some unknown reason. In this instance, *Train Nutter*, started off on the seat parallel to Jeff and I. *Train Nutter,* fixed his gaze on me, an after an uncomfortable amount of time, my husband suggested I swap seats with him so that *Train Nutter* was affectively seated across the aisle from him, not me. *Train Nutter* then proceeded to empty the contents of his plastic bag, out onto the table and look for something to eat, all the while, staring at me and muttering to himself. After Jeff told him to stop, he collected some of this debris, put it in his bag, and moved to another seat. This time, next to a girl and boy of about seventeen, he then proceeded to do the same thing, mumbling in a weird voice, the sort I have heard in French horror films that I have been unfortunate to have played in close proximity to me, by our daughter and her French friends when they used to holiday on our previous boat *Maranatha.*

The girl and boy were laughing, but when the boy got off the train, leaving her alone, she wasn't quite so cocky. Another girl got on the train and the two were whispering, obviously discussing *Train Nutter,* who for the duration had continued to mutter but his behaviour seemed to become more erratic. Plucking up the courage, one of the girls left the carriage to return with a female guard, after some arguing from *Train Nutter*, he gathered his belongings and was escorted from the carriage to stand in the corridor. At the next stop, he was ejected from the train. As it pulled away from the station, he shook his fists. Then the nervous laughter started. By a stroke of luck, he didn't have a ticket, I am unsure whether she would have been able to eject him in other circumstances, but relieved he had gone. I did feel a bit edgy the rest of the day, re living his creepy voice in my head. I just hoped we wouldn't seem him somewhere we stop, canals after all are rife with nutters, some of us even live on boats!

The night before we left, we called to say goodbye to Sally and Glenn and fortunately, they went through the map telling us where we could stop, and where was nice. It's one of those things that we all do, pointing out potential dangers, and we were certainly pleased we had consulted them we were arrived in Toulouse to a rather nasty current. So, our last night, was spent, like many other nights in Castelnaudary, with Sally and Glenn, a large carafe of wine and *Haggis* nuzzling me.

It's always sad leaving somewhere you have stayed for a while, the little old lady, that I had talked to every morning since our first day, albeit, she may not have understood me, came down to say goodbye. I hoped the next people that moored there was as friendly, we had been there for six weeks, and become part of her routine to stop and chat on the way to and from the shops. I had said goodbye to the old men that played petanque, I suppose for them, these strange people that come and go are part of their daily back drop, as they became part of ours.

Our first few days, cruising in the glorious autumn weather was superb, it had been the longest time we had stayed in one place and we were itching to get on our way. The hordes of hire boats had marginally diminished, leaving more private boats making their last trip of the season. The normal lock keepers seemed refreshed after their summer vacation, although after a few days we were on automated locks, with the freedom to start and finish when we wanted. Several days into cruising, we had the pleasure of purchasing some fresh figs from one of the lock keepers. I wasn't even sure whether I liked figs, they aren't exactly something on the daily menu growing up in the North East of England, but it would have been rude to refuse when he proffered a brimming bowl, as we entered the lock. Calling upon my mother's culinary expertise, I telephoned her and asked for her recommendations for what to eat with figs. Cheese and wine was the response! I could have worked that one out for myself. It was the following year, when I had purchased some figs, sadly from a supermarket, when I realised that she didn't actually like figs, hence the lack of enthusiasm. It was a bit of a blow as I was attempting to recreate a splendid platter of figs, Parma ham and fresh leaves that her best friend Pauline had prepared for us for dinner. It was absolutely delicious, but nothing is ever as good if you make it yourself. It seemed that I had rather a lot of figs, and after a few days, and a look online for recipes, I found one in my old Jamie Oliver Cookbook, with pork. Luckily, I had a piece of pork in the freezer, so the next day, I slow cooked my pork with quite a lot of figs, it was mouth-watering. I have since become I vegetarian, so will not be reconstructing the dish, I don't think tofu would taste as good, however as it is highly unlikely I should find myself with another bowl of figs, I don't need to worry. Should I do, they are delicious with goat's cheese, and wine, obviously.

When we left the land of lock keepers, the joys of not having a lock keeper to keep us to schedule, we soon outweighed by the inconvenience of having to slow down, get off and open the lock, then try and jump back on as the lock went down. The first few locks had nasty outflows, so as Jeff tried to stop for me to alight, he was pushed sideways, regaining position then seemed to send him at a funny angle. Various tactics were employed until we managed to get in relatively straight. To a narrow boater reading this, they would probably think, what is all the fuss about, having to get off the boat, but we are spoilt in France, a swizzle stick to activate the lock opening, or even better, a remote to open it is a lot easier than trying to get on and off. We soon realised that the best method was for me to get off on the side of the waiting pontoon, walk to the lock and then walk across the lock gates to activate the lock, then jump on as quick as possible, it was keeping me fit anyway, after weeks of sitting about when it was too hot.

 By day Four, we stopped at the most charming spot, a duck house was adjacent to the mooring. We arrived just before midday on a Sunday morning, and I dashed into the village to get bread before the boulangerie closed. I don't know what it is about boating, I don't think I have ever eaten so much bread, but there is a Pavlov's dog reaction. As soon as we moor, I much go searching for bread. I think I have been in France too long! Years ago, we were having a barbeque and I my French friends told us, we had not bought enough bread, to me there was quite enough, but that was before I realised that they wouldn't really eat the salad I had made, a barbeque in France is baguette and meat, enough of both to make your stomach groan, obviously washed down with copious amounts of wine.

As I walked back from the village, I noticed a garage with classic cars parked outside. After lunch, we would investigate further. Towards the end of the day, a homemade electric boat arrived with a solo passenger. The man was trying to raise money for Cancer Research, with the intention of travelling the Midi. Unfortunately, we had only seen one place along the way between here and Castelnaudary with electricity, he had travelled one day from Toulouse and already found that he was moored without electricity. Perhaps starting further along the canal would have been a better idea as the frequency of stops with power for a tiny boat were regular. We went to sleep that night to the dulcet sounds of his generator running, but without it, he wouldn't get far the following day.

Bilbo was sad to leave as he had spent the afternoon watching the ducks gathered in their duck house with fascination, so many ducks in one place. Poor *Matilda* had had to remain indoors, and the mooring was adjacent to the main thoroughfare to Toulouse. It being Sunday, the dog walkers and families were out in full and for some reason, unbeknownst to me, each person, felt it necessary to cross the road and walk down the bank onto the stretch where our boat was moored, stepping over the lines, peering into the boat. I had spent the afternoon fending off curious dogs, eager to leap aboard. Definitely not a good idea with our vicious tiger aboard, or her sometimes protectorate.

...ning, and we were travelling through the centre of Toulouse, ...y uninspiring day with a little drizzle. Passing by the main port, ... Saveur, stuffed with boats of all shaped and sizes, I was interested to see giant banners of Rugby players. The Irish pub, situated close to the quay, was showing all the televised matches of the Rugby World Cup that was about to take place. These locks were all controlled by a watch tower and CCTV, so we had little to do except get into the correct position and indicate we were ready. We had a French couple in the lock behind us, and their little dog ran up and down the boat barking throughout the experience, making me nervous for its safety and lack concentration. I didn't get a feel of Toulouse, the locks are in an area with offices on one side and the train station on the other, with trees lining them, I am sure had the sun been shining it would have been a different experience, but I imagine in the summer, the shelter would be gratefully appreciated.

Leaving Toulouse, you enter a narrow stretch leading to a stretch of water with a small mooring and entrance to the Canal de Brienne and the Canal de Garonne. We had been warned by Glenn that the current was strong, and he wasn't kidding. It was a struggle to get into position, even with our heavy boat, as we entered the Garonne passage the first thing we saw were the belongings of someone sleeping rough. As with all cities it is not unusual but nether less always saddening, with a city with some much wealth and opportunity, a centre of technological excellence, where Airbus, Concorde and the Hermes Space Shuttle originate, there is still poverty. Leaving Toulouse, we passed shanty towns, the less beautiful boats situated on the outskirts, adjacent to gypsy camps. But next to that, a canoeing club, life existing side by side. A floating bridge across the canal to the famous football stadium, the Stade de Toulouse, stops navigation during big matches, we passed through in this instance, another time. We were now on the last canal of the year, The Canal de

Garonne, minimal hire boats this end, and hopefully some lovely scenery as we were entering the fruit growing region.

We were aware that along the stretch heading out of Toulouse were several dealerships selling motorhomes, stopping on a tiny overgrown pontoon, we walked through knee high grass and nettles to get to the next lock and onto the main road, The Avenue Unites Etats, possibly the busiest road in Southern France! With little footpath, we were taking our life into our own hands but our idea to tentatively look at motorhomes had been growing over the last few weeks, since the dreadful night in the caravan. After visiting the three shops along situated along the road, we were had a better idea of the models on offer and arriving back at the boat, we almost convinced that we should buy one and sell the caravan., it was fortunate that we had more travelling to do to prevent us from buying one straight away, as we are rather impulsive. With trains hurtling passed us regularly, the canal de Garonne runs parallel to train line, we were not going to get much sleep, but my head was full of new adventures to be head, on the road, rather than the water.

Our second night on the Garonne brought us to St Jory, still near Toulouse, but a much more pleasant mooring, situated next to the cycle track. We were tied up on metal shuttering, the metal bits have holes for you to put the ropes through, we were a little dubious, but they seemed to hold. A peaceful spot away from the train and importantly, somewhere we could let *Matilda* out. She quickly found shade in the adjacent woods and remained there until late that evening. When an English boat arrived later that afternoon, of similar style to ours, we advised them that there was a possibility she may try to get on their boat in confusion. They laughed and said they would bring her back if she did. They were travelling back the route we had taken, with the intention of heading North back to the Rhone and the Saone to return to Auxonne for the winter. Their comment that they didn't like it in the South, because non-one went anywhere, was interesting, so far, we had found that there were pockets of communities and not a great deal of cruising occurring, but the combination of searing heat, lack of mooring for the bigger boats, and rising fuel costs were perhaps the reason. Some people are happy to be on their boats with good company, at the moment we were keen to cruise as we had been waiting years to do it unfettered but at some stage the novelty may wear off, but not at the moment.

The following morning, feeling refreshed after a decent night's sleep and a tranquil walk with *Bilbo*, we set off for the day. Usually, before we leave I make sure that *Matilda* is in our bedroom with the door closed. The tendency to bolt at the sound of the engine starting up has caused this action. This particular morning, Jeff was trying to get the ropes through the shuttering to release us, as I returned with *Bilbo*, quickly putting him inside, we cast off. It was shortly afterwards that I realised that I couldn't find *Matilda*. Notifying the Captain, he pulled over to the side of the canal and I hopped off. Forty-five minutes later I still hadn't found her, and it was not possible for the boat to moor as the edges were too shallow. Jeff had reversed the boat backwards as best he could. Hysterical, I got back onto the boat, suggesting that we tried to get to the next available mooring and then cycle back and search for her. As we approached the lock, I dashed back into the boat to get a drink and there she was sitting on the chair. It was the second time a week she had disappeared in the morning, the first day away from Castelnaudary we had moored next to the tow path and she had tootled off into the woods, obviously sulking at being kept indoors for weeks, she had stayed out all night. After Jeff unsuccessfully finding her, *Bilbo* and I took over the reins. My combination of singing, and dancing about, which made *Bilbo* bark, I assume waking her from wherever she had hidden. She slunk back nonchantly. We definitely needed to keep her in more, I couldn't cope with the stress.

The back drop grew greener and we were soon in the village of Grissoles. There are two moorings there. One in a cut out, which was full, and another, further along with space for a couple of boats. There was already one tied up and we moored in front of it. The first mooring was more sheltered, with a manicured area in front but as we were relying on our solar power, we were happy to stop in the more exposed place. With a boulangerie within walking distance I was happy, another ghost town with a spanking new village hall and a spot behind it for motorhomes. We watched as they lined up for the evening, the following morning we would see the owners all trotting to the boulangerie to stock up for the day, I swear we are all brainwashed, we must eat bread.

As we tied up, a lady sat on the bench in front of the boat. She sat there on her own all afternoon. After dark, the lights were illuminated on the boat next to us. After much giggling, all went dark on the small boat. Sometime later, they came back on, and a man and a woman exited, it appeared that the owner was using his boat for romantic liaisons!

Our next stop was in Montech. We didn't take the water slope, which was adjacent to the lock and whilst we were there we did not see it in operation, but it certainly was an interesting piece of machinery. To allow the boat to ascend a moveable gate is lifted, the boat enters then the gate is lowered, the boat is then floating on a wedge of water, I would have loved to see it in action, but thanks to Rick Stein, I have seen it on his DVD. Personally, I was pleased we were going through a normal lock. As we exited the lock we tied up to a single mooring. It was perfect, secluded and no road access. We let *Matilda* out and after a walk let *Bilbo* outside as there was a stone table and chairs next to the stone pontoon. Jeff sat outside with him, enjoying the Autumn sunshine and a cup of tea, and I was just changing into some shorts when a little white van appeared, driving across the wasteland. It stopped and two men in hunting clothing got out, letting out two hunting dogs. Luckily, *Matilda* was not far away, and I quickly grabbed hold of her and much to her annoyance, shut her inside. Jeff took *Bilbo* back onto the boat and the men settled onto the table, for the duration of the afternoon, so much for our tranquillity. Poor

Bilbo was beside himself, two dogs loose, right next to him, they proceeded to howl their way through the afternoon, evidently disgruntled that they were not getting any action, their owners obviously sloping off from home, under the pretence of going hunting and just wanted a chat!

Perhaps half an hour after they had left, I was just getting *Bilbo* off the boat to take him for a walk when Lynda and Steve arrived with *Rollo*. As soon as they were rafted to us, the only way to moor with limited space, *Rollo* leapt onto our boat and we let he and *Bilbo* off to dash around together, *Bilbo* as ever lying on the ground to let *Rollo* nibble him, a peculiar thing he used to do with *Billy*, back when we were in Froncles. Lynda and Steve were both exhausted as they were travelling much further than us. They had booked their boat further along the canal than us and needed to get there before the port closed mid-October. They headed off before us, *Rollo* running up and down the boat as they pulled away, he was sorry to say goodbye to his French friend, but there would always be next year to get into scrapes together.

We arrived later that day at Castelsarrasin mid-afternoon. We were moored away from the port and after tying up securely decided to walk up to port with *Bilbo* and have a look around. The entrance to the port had boats moored along to quay, and as we approached, a German Shepherd dog jumped off an old hire boat, and attacked *Bilbo*. Jeff had to shoo the dog away, whilst I tried to walk backwards away from the dog. Not a great welcome, my poor fur baby was terrified. The dog then jumped back on the boat, presumably ready for the next person/dog to terrorise, walking along a public footpath.

The actual port was at the end of the quay, and all the pontoons were full, the café, that I understood had just opened was bustling but I was not in a mood to sit and enjoy the September sun, my poor dog was looking around for his attacker. After a reasonable walk, we returned to our boat, avoiding the side of the quay, I walked in the opposite direction later that evening. So, my first impressions of Castelsarrasin were not good, perhaps my expectations are too high. We would be in Moissac the next day, where we would moor for the winter, in the pretty town mooring, surrounding by charming houses rather than low rent accommodation.

We were a day earlier than expected, so I made a phone call to Karen at Moissac and asked if we could come in early. With busy ports this is always advisable, and we had expected to stay in Castelsarrasin for a couple of days. But I saw nothing worth staying for. Our last day cruising for the year, would be on the one of the last glorious days of autumn, before winter gales would rob the trees of leaves and the icy gales would blow them into the canal, leaving a thick carpet in the water, to block boat filters and leave the ground slippery underfoot. Or so we thought.

Our first views of Moissac were truly stunning, there is a channel of water across a bridge, the aqueduct, and the views were simply magnificent. The first lock was manned by the lock VNF and upon exiting, we went under a modern metal bridge, then we were there, in port, in our final destination for the year. In seven months we had travelled from one end of France to the other, and seen some amazing sights, and met some wonderful people along the way.

Arriving in port we went straight into our winter spot. With electricity not absolutely essential we were tucked at the end of the quay. Our electric cables reached anyway but we were warned that around the time everyone commences cooking there evening meals there could be a surge and the power could trip. As, all our cooking was electric, we used our solar reserves during the day, and switched over to mains at night which solved the potential problem, as long as the sun shone! As soon as we settled into our spot, we drove to Toulouse and returned to the motorhome shops we had visited the previous week, and arranged to buy one. It seemed too easy, as the salesman spoke very good English. After our misunderstanding with the caravan (or the salesman's ineptitude, confirming that it had, in fact got hot water, to then find out when we drove for six hours to collect it, that it hadn't) we were relieved to be dealing with someone we could communicate with efficiently. Having the ability to argue with officials in French about the reams of paperwork they issue, is not the same as buying something, it was considerably more money than a caravan, as you would expect, this time there was no room for mistakes. We left a deposit, and then returned to Moissac, to ask Iain, the then Captain, if it was ok if we could park it in front of our boat when it arrived. The boat next to us had a motorhome parked outside, and the following week, another couple arrived in their motorhome, to stay on their boat, and it seemed to be quite a common thing amongst boaters, the freedom to travel all year.

With the motorhome due for collection in the next couple of weeks, we had more urgent matters to attend to. We needed to sell the caravan. A garbled phone call, my French still appeared to be appalling, and we arranged to collect the caravan from its winter storage. So, we drove back to Castelnaudary, stopping and having lunch at the same benches we watched people eat at from our boat every day. We took *Bilbo* for a walk around the port, but all our friends had departed. Sally and Glenn were on the way to Toulouse to have some work done on their boat, joining us later in Moissac, everyone else had gone to Carcassonne, as the port of Castelnaudary was being drained that winter so was closed, all must evacuate.

We collected the caravan much to the bewilderment of the man who owned the storage barns. We had signed a contract for twelve months, and it had been there, one. We explained that we were buying a 'camping car' the French term for a motorhome, and we would bring it back for storage in March, to remain there for the summer, most French people store them for the winter and use them for the summer, so I think he saw that as a perfect solution, he could rent our space out for the winter and get paid twice!

We parked the caravan in front of the boat for a day, and gave it a good clean, then took it to a campsite in a nearby village, unfortunately, the local one was already closed for the season, it wasn't even the half term holidays yet, but in France, even in the South, they shut early. We arranged to leave it there for a week, with the hope it was sold by then, and took some photos for an advertisement and returned to our boat. Within a day, someone had responded to our advertisement on Bon coin, the French equivalent of Gum Tree, and we had a viewing. We also received lots of text and phone calls, that resulting in one lady, shouting down the phone that I must not sell it to anyone else, she must have it! We were a tad concerned, as we were aware that French gyspies tend to buy caravans in France, and without any friends around, we were putting ourselves into a vulnerable situation.

We judged that the man that turned up seemed reasonably ok. One of the things that indicated whether they were gyspies was trying to pay cash, apart from anything, you cannot pay cash into a bank without a good reason, and who knows where the money could have come from. The second, was we discovered, that our bank, which we had dealt with for years, was not national. Although, you can go to the bank and withdraw money and receive balances, I couldn't pay eight euros in, never mind eight thousand. The chap left with our details, and we arranged for him to collect in in a few days, hoping that it was legitimate. One thing that we had learnt which was superb about the French bank system, is that you cannot stop a cheque, or reverse a bank payment, it is not legal. Years ago, we had bought an infrared sauna for our town house, when it arrived it was faulty, I went to the bank and asked them to stop the payment as the company were not answering their phones, the bank told me I would have to take legal action to get the money back. In that instance, it worked against us, although eventually we got hold of them and they sent some replacement parts, but certainly when you are selling something privately, you are protected. Once the money is in your account, it is staying put.

The man took his caravan away, very happy and so were we, it had been a reasonably unstressful procedure, and we had learnt an expensive mistake, ask many questions when you are buying something and get a written specification. The advert stating that it had hot water, had of course disappeared as soon as we had paid a deposit. A lesson learnt the hard way.

With a wait for our motorhome, and fantastic autumn weather, we went through the double lock onto the Tarn river leading from the port. There were several other boats moored there and the views onto the river were wonderful. A large bridge stretched across which was lit up at night and a hotel and Spa, Le *Moulin de Moissac* overlooked it, throwing out light into the night. What I was surprised about was that the lights remained on all night, and apart from people wandering down to fish, it seemed reasonably quiet there. One thing that was particularly convenient was the location in relation to the bar, where *Friday Night Drinks* took place *The Sunbeam*. The bar was named such, as half a Sunbeam car was attached to the wall in the bar! The captains of the port, Iain and Karen Noble, had made it a tradition that every Friday evening at Six o'clock, the boaters went down to The Sunbeam for a social. Jackie the owner provided splendid frites with the drinks and pizzas were available to order. Usually by nine everyone had gone home, I soon learned after the first week to eat before we went, as we inevitably ended up talking and by the time we had taken *Bilbo* for a walk it was too late to eat, frites are nice but not dinner! It was a great opportunity to get to know the regulars of the port. Each week new people arrived and contrary to the comments of the couple we had met the previous week, people did cruise around in the South, I think that it was the Midi that was the problem, with overcrowding from hire boats and the assisted locks a deterrent. Here, it seemed that everyone had just returned from somewhere, and were keen to discuss their adventures. What was also great, wasn't all ex pats attending, some of the local French attended, and English people that had settled nearby, the port attracted different nationalities, and for the first time since leaving St Jean de Losne, there was a mixture of French, English, Dutch, German, American and Australian Boaters but unlike St Jean de Losne, they were all mixing together, rather than staying in their' tribes'.

We also found that several of the boaters moored along the wall had motorhomes, and were about to pack up for the winter and head to Portugal. It seemed we had the right idea. The first four weeks we were fortunate enough to have weather warm enough to sit outside, it seemed that no one else used the bar, probably as it was situated on the edge of town, so for one night a week the boaters took over for a few hours. What we soon established, was that the majority of boaters, kept their boats in Moissac but went home, or away. The Californians moored next to us were off to Italy for the winter, another couple were going to Brittany, which is really the next county, what we realised is by the end of the month, there would be the Captain and his wife, another two couples, a lone Frenchman and us. I was pleased that we were heading off but knew that Sally and Glenn would not be impressed when they arrived, and the port was deserted.

After a trip up to Toulouse to check a few things about our impending purchase, we were dismayed to discover that the English-speaking sales man, had all but disappeared. He had been covering from another office, we were left again with only French speakers, we prayed that this time there would not be a problem. I spent a few days trying to track him down, but he seemed to have vanished into thin air. The same thing happened a few years previously, when we purchased our last boat, *Maranatha*, a young blonde Adonis, had helped us with the sale, allegedly the son of the owner, when we returned to Holland, after paying the deposit, he had left the company. We had no end of trouble with the boat, lost paperwork and a bill for a tax account to get us a tax certificate so we could ship it out of the country. This did not bode well.

We decided to take advantage of the good weather and buy some paint for the roof of the boat, it was a dull bone colour and our new burgundy on the sides, did not pop. It was the perfect situation to paint as the trees were much further back than in the port, and we had been moored close by to some horse chestnut trees. In the evening, Iain, the Captain, would take his dog *Ziggy*, a gorgeous Dalmatian for a security walk around the port, often tossing conkers for *Ziggy* to chase, I soon got used to the sound of them clunking against the boat, or the splash into the water. The leaves were playing havoc with our pale grey deck and we seemed to be walking gravel in continuously, so our choice of mooring on the river was a great improvement, it was a shame we couldn't stay there permanently but as the river had a tendency to flood it was not possible.

We were used to people walking past an admiring our boat, it is rather like having a classic car, people want to ask you about it. It is a good chance for Jeff to practice his French and we all like to be admired, even if it's just our paintwork! With the work completed, a lady stopped and opening with a compliment of the boat, she then changed tack and asked us if she could photograph the boat. This is not an unusual request, when we are moving, it can be photographed each day, but her request was unique. She enquired if it was possible for a charity calendar to be shot on our boat. She explained that she worked for a local company *'Bout du Nez'*, who provided entertainment for older people in institutions, hospitals and ill children. I replied that I didn't see why not, but conferred with Jeff, who agreed with me that it wouldn't be a problem and arranged for her to come back the following week.

One of the boaters, Gill and I had been chatting, and as a keen photographer, she was showing me some of the shots she had taken recently, including the local homeless man, who we named *Cat Man*, as he carried a knapsack on his back with kittens in it. *Cat Man* lived in a tent along the river, and Gill had discovered him one day, listening to classical music, his cd player plugged into an electrical point provided by outdoor concerts. He obviously also had the password to the Wi-Fi at the hotel as he had his laptop was also plugged in. As I am always wandering around with *Bilbo* I soon discovered *Cat Man* and his tent, but was fascinated that Gill had seen insight into his world. That is the eye of a good photographer. I started to see *Cat Man*, all over Moissac after that, in the supermarket, with his bag of cats outside, in front of the Abbaye, in the centre of town, I suppose once I disassociated him from being in the tent, I had opened my eyes, or rather Gill had! When I explained to Gill that there was a photoshoot occurring the following week, she arrived the day of the shoot, with her camera, hoping to watch them in action, and take a photo if permitted.

Jeff had cleaned the boat and it was gleaming. First the photographer arrived, then the local paper, then the lady I had spoken to, then the clowns. Yes, I had agreed to a troop of clowns, posing on our boat for their Christmas calendar!

In the meantime, the photographer had been conversing with Gill and arranged for her to take some shots too and she would meet up with him later and copy them, a professional assignment.

For several hours, music was played, and the clowns danced on the freshly painted roof of our boat, the dual concern for health and safety and the welfare of my very old boat causing me to call out at regular intervals to be careful. At the point when they were jumping up and down on the roof, Jeff went inside, under the pretence of calming *Bilbo* from the banging, but he was also becoming anxious. As the sun started to fade, they called a halt and one by one alighted. It was certainly a memorable day, I don't know anyone else who has had dancing clowns on their roof, or are likely to. The joy of having a boat, unexpected experiences.

Photo taken by Gill Pavitt

With our motorhome's arrival imminent, we decided to return through the two locks to port. Our friends Donna and Darren were due to arrive in a week and we intended on using it for the duration as their holiday accommodation, allowing them some privacy, on a week away from their two teenage sons. When we went to collect the motorhome, luckily there wasn't any problems. Jeff had the experience of driving a manual left-hand drive vehicle for the first time in years, onto one of the busiest roads in the South, the Avenue United Etats, and I had the joy of following him, having not driven further than the supermarket in Castelnaudary for the past few months. Throwing myself driving headlong into heavy traffic was not a pleasant experience, but at least I was used to driving Jeff's car. He was getting to grips with a bone shaking motorhome. Fortunately, as it was on a Mercedes Chassis, it was of good quality, but that didn't stop it rattling and sounding like he was driving an old van.

We parked up outside the boat, and I fiddled around inside, making lists of things we needed to buy. Also, a good excuse for a shop. The following day, we were back in Toulouse, ordering an awning, and buying a cooker and a stand for the 'outside kitchen'. We had a pitch booked on a site in Spain for December and an appointment to get a bar fitted to the motorhome for the awning. I was excited with all my new purchases and the impending holiday. We had no idea what we would do in January, but our daughter was booked on a flight to Alicante for Christmas and we would be spending New Year in Spain. Not much to complain about there.

The end of the week, we were at Toulouse airport collecting Donna and Darren. Darren is a keen angler, and Jeff had taken the opportunity of his impending arrival to test the waters around the boat, on the river. That evening, as it was Friday, we took our friends to The Sunbeam for a drink before dinner, then returned to the boat to the *Coq au Vin*, I had prepared earlier. They snuggled down for the night in our new motorhome, parked outside our boat. After breakfast onboard, *Bilbo* and I had walked up to town to *Intermarche* to buy croissants, which conveniently has an outside boulangerie, perfect with a dog in tow. I had booked to go through the locks again, we were becoming familiar figures with the local VNF men. Darren helped with the locks, Donna had done her fair share over the years on *Maranatha* and had arrived on holiday with immaculately manicured nails, we didn't need her to help and it would have been unfair to ask.

With only one other boat on the quay, it was the perfect place to spend the week. We were treated to a last-minute blast of sunshine and were able to set our chairs on the quay. As *Bilbo* was also outside, *Oscar*, the West Highland Terrier, would trot down regularly to say Hello. While we relaxed, Darren and Jeff set the fishing rods up and took our small boat into the water. Saturday, being the day that the trip boat at the end of the quay was in operation, was perhaps not the best choice to start fishing, as the boat kept crossing the fishing lines, so they gave up until later in the week. Sunday is market day in Moissac, and as we had walked into town to do some sightseeing on Saturday afternoon, but the warmth of the day had disappeared and after admiring the medieval Saint Pierre Abbey, another world heritage site, we returned to the boat, not suitably attired to sip wine, or even coffee as the autumn winds whipped around us.

Waking to another bright morning, we walked to the market, not because I thought they would possibly want to buy anything, but merely for the experience. The market in Moissac, is much larger than our local market in Vitry le Francois, which Donna had visited many times over the years with the children in tow, usually to buy tat that the boys wanted or delicious rotisserie chicken for lunch with fresh baguette for lunch.

The market in Moissac, reflected the ethnicity of the area, with a large Muslim population, one section of the market sold products specifically aimed at their requirements a pocket of a different culture, with food stalls, clothing, and soft furniture's, it was fascinating, small boys played on the ground in front of the stalls, it was like being transported to a different country, yet in the middle of France. To people who live in certain parts of England, I expect this is not unusual sight, but Vitry was a hotpotch of ethnicity but it was the obvious segregation that I found startling in Moissac. It would be something that I would become more aware of during our stay there.

The first week we had arrived I had gone to the market, and been delighted at the array of fresh food available, the town was the busiest I had seen it, all the cafes were full, and the shops, that barely seemed to have customers were bustling, the town had come alive. Attending the market was obviously a day out. It soon became a weekly part of my routine, stopping off at the boulangerie to buy some delicious cakes on the way back and of course, some bread. In a short time, I felt very at home in Moissac, the combination of the beautiful surroundings, the little art gallery to admire on the walk into town, the smart cafes and restaurants and the Italian Deli nestled amongst the Glass wear shops and tourist shop, the wonderful walks with *Bilbo*, along the banks of the Tarn, it was all perfect. Within a few days I had interacted with the locals, I had a lady with a limp, who stopped to stroke *Bilbo*, and various dog walkers who dogs became doggie friends, and a few that weren't, like the nasty Jack Russell that I had been warned about by Karen, who not only would attack Bilbo, but probably me too, as he had harassed *Ziggy* previously.

With regard to another vicious dog, when we arrived, I related the story of Castelsarrasin to Karen, and she said, that the dog belonged to someone they knew, and that she was harmless. The following day, I walked to the port office with *Bilbo*, and the German Shepherd dashed out and ran at *Bilbo*, this time I was prepared, and as we quickly returned to our boat she ran off. The dog obviously did not like *Bilbo*, it's strange that she reacted the same way again, but perhaps she felt that the office was her territory too. I soon learned which car belonged to its owner, who frequently popped over to do 'jobs 'in the port, and kept *Bilbo* inside in case she was there. Unfortunately, it gave *Bilbo* an aversion to German Shepherds, which was a shame, as someone owned one locally and walked it along the quay every day, and it of course stopped next to our boat for a sniff, usually causing *Matilda* to hiss and jump onto the boat, and *Bilbo* to emit a low growl, most unlike him.

As Moissac is a predominate region for fruit growing, we found that a house opposite the port, was home to seasonal fruit pickers. On Saturday around Midday, obviously their day off, the music would commence, the windows would be opened, and we were all treated to some extraordinary sounds, until around Six in the evening when the music would stop. When we returned after our winter break ,there were new families living there, different children playing in the street, what happened to the children and school goodness knows, but I couldn't understand, in a country with such a high level of unemployment why it was necessary to bring people in to do the jobs, but with the movement of people in Europe, it makes it a lot easier, and if the French want to stay at home, and claim unemployment benefit then we can only support those people who make the effort. Living in a country where you don't speak the language is incredibly hard, but as English expats, we generally receive a warm reception, unless of course we try and set a business up, as we did. Migrant workers live on the outside of society and certainly the French don't want them there, but they do want their strawberries picked, so they have no choice. With the Brexit vote the following summer, perhaps the Uk will have fields of rotting crops, when the country decides they want to stop migrant workers coming and it will become a more common sight in France. Perhaps we won't be there to see what happens, as after all, we too, are guests in the Country and may have no rights to float around Europe freely on our boats, as we are fortunate enough to do now.

After an enjoyable week, with Donna and Darren, the first time they had ever visited, when we didn't need to dash off to work, we dropped them off in Toulouse to spend the day sightseeing before their flights. After a week of glorious sunshine, the clouds opened, and they spent a damp soggy day appreciating the fine city. As it was now the end of October, it was time for Karen and Iain to remove the pontoons on the other side of the river. We had not moored on them as the boat was too heavy, and the quay was preferable for us. It was quite a big job, as the electricity needed to be disconnected and the water, but the river undoubtedly would flood over the winter and it was a yearly necessity. As we returned our boat to the port, they disassembled the floating pontoons and brought them round to the front of where our boat was moored, they were chained up and would remain there until at least May.

We started to slowly, "put our boat to bed for the winter," the yearly jobs necessary before you leave your boat. As we would not be cruising until the Spring, lifejackets were cleaned and put away, coats washed, and winter clothes unpacked. We were hoping that we wouldn't have need of a lot of our winter clothes this year as we were heading to Spain, but it still gets cold at night. Meanwhile, Sally and Glenn arrived finally, after a delay in dry dock in Toulouse, the sound of *Haggis* and *Deliah* barking outside the boat alerted us to their presence and soon it became a daily ritual as Sally took them for their walk, via us, so we could join them.

Bilbo does not walk well on the lead and Jim, one of the residents on another boat, had bought a harness for *Bella* his Labrador cross. It seemed to the do the trick, so I ordered one from EBay, and within a couple of had days *Bilbo*'s arrived. He was not impressed with the paraphernalia strapped to him but did appear to walk better, and been making progress with him when Sally and Glenn arrived in port. Walking with Sally is always fun but quite tiring, *Haggis* is a natural swimmer, and jumps into the canal at the first instance, *Deliah* is a little more reticent. Walking with them, Sally had different demands from the two dogs, *Haggis* wanted stones in the water, to swim to, *Deliah* wanted balls and sticks to chase. *Bilbo*, only ever wants to chase something if it belongs to someone else, unless it is a cat. We were having a lovely winter walk, Sandra, *Bella's* 'mum' had joined us somewhere along the canal, and *Deliah, Bilbo* and *Bella* were dashing around chasing sticks, *Bilbo* was still on his harness and Sally urged me to take it off, so he could run more freely. *Bilbo* is incredibly naughty and runs off in the opposite direction in the first instance, many times on walks with *Haggis* and *Deliah*, he has disappeared, and we have found him in someone's allotment or he has run off away from the pack in search of something. I only wish we had lived in the Uk when he was a puppy and I could have taken him to training classes but apparently it is in his genealogy, his breed are notoriously difficult to train, he is however a lovely good-natured boy, so I can't complain, having had a German Shepherd previously who wanted to eat everybody, to have my cartoon character of a dog, that little children want to cuddle, is not such a bad thing, especially living the lifestyle that we do.

As we approached the aqueduct across the river, *Haggis* was swimming, as usual, and foolishly I removed *Bilbo's* harness, he doesn't like *Haggis* swimming, he can't understand that his little friend is not in danger, and tends to run up and down the bank and bark in distress. One-minute *Bilbo* was barking, the three of us where chatting and *Bella* and *Deliah* were hurtling up and down the path, the next the barking stopped, and I looked round and said

"Where's *Bilbo*".

We looked towards the other dogs and then realised he had fallen in the aqueduct, possibly the worse place as the flat sides would prevent him getting out. Sally threw herself on the ground and grabbed hold of him as he was floundering in the margins, letting out his distress call. I knelt down and grabbed hold of Sally. She is a strong, fit lady as she still plays in Netball tournaments, there wasn't a snowballs chance in hell, I could have pulled him in myself, but my job was to stop Sally falling in, while she pulled him. She yanked him up out of the water, onto the path and he shook himself off and wagged his tale. I put his harness on quickly. Had I not removed it in the first place, it would have been easy to get him out, as the *Julius Harness*, comes with a grab handle on top, very handy at steering him out of the way when old ladies pass, and obviously an asset when your dog is drowning. Had Sally not been there, he would have drowned, and so perhaps may I, trying to save him.

The first Friday night that Sally and Glenn were in port, *The Sunbeam*, was packed. We had tried the pizza's the previous week and I wasn't keen, but we ended up staying anyway and ordering one, with two dogs waiting for any left overs, there was not a waste. On Sundays I cooked, it was a nice end to the weekend, and a chance to put the world right. By the second weekend, Friday night drinks the port was deserted. Karen and Iain had gone on holiday, and there were eight of us. It was hardly worth him opening the bar. It was a sign of the winter to come, we were glad we would be leaving soon. The following week, Sally invited some friends over from another port, Montauban, only one half of the couple came, but there were three car loads of them, and a good excuse to meet more likeminded people. It was an entertaining evening, and whilst we were in Spain, the two groups regularly joined forces to keep everyone sane on the long winter nights.

After having a new piece fitted onto our motorhome, we packed up and headed off to Spain, in search of sun. Moissac, was a charming town, but by the end of November, the days were long and grey, the morning mist took until lunchtime to clear. We had been fortunate that most of the month the weather had been unusually warm, it wasn't until the last Sunday in November, that we admitted defeat, and moved our table into the wheelhouse to eat, we had managed dine on the deck, under cover every week until then. It had been over twelve months since we had sold our home and business and waved goodbye to all that was familiar. In the last nine months we had seen vineyards and olive groves, fields of sunflowers and fairy tale castles, now was time for a little rest to recap on our year and plan our next year cruising aboard *Jantina*.

Epilogue

We had barely got to Toulouse when we suddenly heard a crunch. We had smashed a wing mirror on the car in the next lane. We pulled over into an adjacent car park, unfortunately timed as the gendarmes were in the middle of evacuating a gypsy camp that had accumulated in front of Aldi supermarket. By a stroke of luck, the lady driver spoke English, but she couldn't comprehend how we had a French motorhome and were English. We showed her our insurance documents, which obviously were French, and she kept repeating that she would ring her insurance agent and ask him what to do as it was English. After some time, the penny dropped, but understandably, we wanted to get on our way and we offered to give her one hundred Euros to buy a new wing mirror. After several phone calls to her husband, she agreed, the was probably worth about five hundred Euros in total. She was flying to China on business the following morning, hence the reason she spoke good English, and was also anxious to get on her way. It was an expensive lesson to learn, and we would not drive through the centre of Toulouse again but use the toll roads, the roads were too narrow and the traffic crazy. Another expensive lesson to learn, but it could have been worse.

We arrived at the campsite late the following morning, the novelty of being able to stop at the Aires, walk *Bilbo* and have a cup of tea apparent. We had travelled through the night, but when we were tired, stopped and had a nap, and of course, being able to use your own toilet instead of the ghastly hole in the ground in French Aires. We had left Moissac on a dark dank afternoon, and arrived in Spain to dazzling sunlight.

We were given the option of six pitches, so we parked up outside and walked *Bilbo* through the site to locate them, choosing the one that should get the most sun. Next to our pitch was a Casa, a mobile holiday home, and as we pulled up the window opened, and a head popped out asking us if we would like a cup of tea. We soon settled in and found the people staying there a friendly bunch. Within a week, my mother came to stay at my uncle's apartment in a nearby town and we enjoyed spending time with them both. After she left we had more opportunity to get to know people on the other pitches and a lovely couple arrived at the pitch behind us, Paul and Glenis. I can only say that their presence made our holiday special.

Our daughter was due to fly out for Christmas and we were due to leave after the New Year, but we were enjoying content where we were. Our daily walks through the orange groves, walks into the town of Alfas de Pi and the ability to get a bus or tram, to the beach or other towns a novelty after rural France, made it an easy decision. We booked to stay another month, perhaps we had travelled enough this year.

As perchance, the owners of *Louisa*, the hotel barge, who we had spent many pleasurable hours with in Castelnaudary, had an apartment in one of the nearby towns so we were able to meet up with them. I was soon falling for the idea of being in Spain, although, I wasn't so keen on emptying the motorhome toilet. We made many friends on site, our three-legged cat was a particular favourite and *Bilbo* soon had markers around the site, where he stopped, and people made a fuss. On Christmas Day, we left to have Christmas lunch at my uncles, leaving *Matilda*, in the capable care of Glenis and Paul, who had adopted her for the holiday. I had dressed in appropriate smart Christmas attire but had had to strip off as soon as I entered the apartment as it was so hot, certainly a novelty! The night before we had been treated to Christmas carols and everyone was dressed in Christmas Jumpers drinking mulled wine, a little bit of our traditions, amidst the Spanish ones.

After New Year and days of fireworks, sending the pets loopy, as the Spanish let them off during the day as well as at night. Jeff and I were walking around the site with *Bilbo*, we were about to be collected by my uncle to go and visit some friends. We passed one of the Casa's and I noticed a for sale notice "En Venta ". We knocked on the door, had a quick look round and explained that we were about to go out for lunch but would be back that evening. It was perfect, three bedrooms, two bathrooms, furnished with leather suites and lovely mosaic terrace tables. We returned from our friends and by eight that evening, we were drinking champagne with the owners, we had arranged to buy it.

The next week was a flurry of activity, organising money transfers, contents lists, and new contracts for site fees. Within a week we had moved in, emptying the contents of the motorhome into the Casa. We returned to France, took the motorhome back and parked it in front of the boat and took our car back, and lots of tools, the deck needed repairing and there were various DIY jobs needed attending to.

When we had completed them, we enjoyed the fruits of our labour then we became bored. Our thoughts drifted back to the previous year when we had considered starting a new business. Our friends came over for dinner and it was during dinner, we had a conversation about the future. We knew we were bored, perhaps we had been too hasty, again.

The following morning, we walked into town, and I bought an A4 notebook. That afternoon, I started writing my first book based on our life in France, *Living his Dream*.